fresh HOPE

...Cleveland

Resources to Help You Navigate through Unsettled Times

NANCI J. GRAVILL

WESTBOW
PRESS
A DIVISION OF THOMAS NELSON

WestBow Press books may be ordered through booksellers or by contacting:

WestBow Press
A Division of Thomas Nelson
1663 Liberty Drive
Bloomington, IN 47403
www.westbowpress.com
1-(866) 928-1240

Because of the dynamic nature of the Internet, any web addresses or links contained in this book may have changed since publication and may no longer be valid. The views expressed in this work are solely those of the author and do not necessarily reflect the views of the publisher, and the publisher hereby disclaims any responsibility for them.

Any people depicted in stock imagery provided by Thinkstock are models, and such images are being used for illustrative purposes only.

Certain stock imagery © Thinkstock.

ISBN: 978-1-4497-3011-6 (sc)
ISBN: 978-1-4497-3010-9 (e)

Library of Congress Control Number: 2011960188

Printed in the United States of America

WestBow Press rev. date: 2/17/2012

To: Devon, Shannon, and Brenna:

You give me lots of reasons to be grateful.

Hope

is the thing with feathers

that perches in the soul

and sings the tune without the words

and never stops at all.

– Emily Dickinson (1830-1886), American poet[1]

Contents

Contents

Illustrations

Preface

An author writes with a specific purpose in mind. He or she hopes the words of his or her manuscript will affect the reader in a certain way. Currently, with our slower economy and many losing their jobs and homes, let me share with you a few of my objectives in writing this book and how you can benefit from this information.

My first objective is to provide you with helpful information. Within these pages is all the information that I gathered from the community, in an effort to help myself through a very involved cancer experience. So, I've personally used all these ideas and suggestions in my own life. And I know they all work – they do provide help!

My second objective is to inspire and motivate you.

Knowing that this information is from my own experience should, on some level, inspire and motivate you, the reader, in your current circumstances. Knowing that I've dealt with difficulties and have come through them should give you hope and confidence that you will come through your situation too!

This book provides you with a place to begin.

More than anything, this information provides a place for you to begin to find answers to your challenges. And if you find that your life has a good flow and you have no pressing issues right now, this information can still provide you with some great ideas. In fact, you may find several things interesting and just want to try them. Or, on the other hand, you may want to share some of these ideas with someone else who needs some help. Either way, you are making an investment in your life.

These ideas can reduce overwhelming feelings and help you overcome inertia, fear, and panic. How can having a body of information at your fingertips like this reduce overwhelming and any other uncomfortable feelings you may be experiencing? It can help you deal with many of your concerns without a lot of hunting and searching, which takes a lot of your valuable time. This information can get you going in a positive direction with ideas and services that have been tried before. Beside all that, I have sifted out all of the dead ends and interacted with friends, pastors, health care professionals, and members of the community to find this information. This book brings you answers. And having answers to your questions will restore your internal balance and bring you a sense of hope. All you need to do now is open the book and begin to find information for your life! And in doing so, your fear and panic will start to fade, and you'll feel more like yourself again.

Some ideas within the pages of this book will help to increase your coping skills. As we all know, life is stressful. And new circumstances can challenge our abilities to manage our time and money. But they can also greatly challenge our ability to cope emotionally. Each one of us utilizes coping skills every day. A coping skill is one's ability to deal with or overcome adversity, disadvantage, or disability without correcting or eliminating the underlying problem.[2] Our ability to cope with our concerns determines how well we function physically, mentally, and emotionally. Coping skills help us manage our lives.

If you are in a job search at this time or struggling with another challenge, it may be a little while before the tide turns for you. So, in that interim period, how will you wait? What will you do? How will you remain positive and upbeat? What types of attitudes will you hang on to? How will you exercise your faith? The plain truth is, how will you cope?

The information in the second part of this book, "Soothing the Soul: Tips for Emotional Well-Being," provides many good ideas that will help you feel better – and cope better. You will find ways to adjust your thinking, healthy eating ideas, how the words you speak affect your life, and many more ideas. This information will help you stay emotionally healthy. That's because with each challenge in life you'll also find there is an emotional component to deal with like fear, worry, uncertainty, or being overwhelmed. The second section therefore shares ideas to help soothe your emotional well-being to help you tackle those emotions. These suggestions will help lift your emotions and increase your ability to cope which will help you get beyond your concerns. My hope is that these Scripturally-based ideas may lead you to discover other ways you can be more resourceful, creative, and engaged in your daily living. Even if you are experiencing many challenges, these ideas will help you enjoy your life and help you stay positive. This information is helpful for anyone at any time.

This information may help you develop other creative ideas. The information and ideas here will help you get started. And by doing so, they will help you build momentum. And as that builds, it will help you think more about your own needs and ultimately help you generate more creative ideas that are well-suited for your life.

The ideas I've presented here may help you start thinking differently about your situation. They may shed new light on how you are living – or how you want to live. The ideas shared here may be things you've never thought of before. They may be, as they say, "outside the box." According to Michael Michalko, in his article, "Thinking Like a Genius: Eight Strategies Used by the Supercreative from Aristotle and Leonardo to Einstein and Edison,"

> Typically, we think reproductively – that is, on the basis of problems encountered in the past. However, geniuses think productively, not reproductively. When confronted with a problem, they ask, "How many ways can I look at it?", "Can I rethink the way I see it?", [and] "How many different ways can I solve it?" [3]

And so, you too may come to realize that thinking differently can have a direct effect on your current situation. Expanding your thinking can help you develop and discover other healthy strategies for your life. But if you always do the same things, you'll always get the same results.

Discovering new ideas can help you increase your sense of satisfaction with your life. That may also increase your overall sense of well-being. And people who are satisfied with their lives more than likely live longer, and I would imagine, experience less depression. So, it's a good thing to explore and remain open to other options for yourself, particularly if your financial situation dictates doing things with a different twist.

A sentence on the previous page of this section contains the word "creative." And I know for many of you, that's a scary thought. But creative ideas and creative thinking aren't necessarily about painting, writing, or dancing. You don't have to have one bit of artistic ability to be creative when it comes to living your life. It's about expanding your thinking -- it's about thinking bigger. Creative thinking is about finding as many answers as you can. And for some of you, that will feel strange, but it can be very freeing as well. So, think a little bigger and see what other great ideas you can find for your life!

These ideas will help you develop other healthy strategies for living. As mentioned earlier, all the information here will introduce you to healthy strategies for living. All you need to do is be open-minded and try them!

This material provides a vehicle to share the love of Christ with others. Sharing this information with the unsaved person is God's love in action.

Use this information as a helpful tool to share Christ with the unsaved. Most of us are aware that it may be a little while before our country pulls through these economic difficulties. And so, what do you hang on to in life if you don't have God?

We all come in contact with people every day, whether we are at the grocery store, car dealership, or talking with a neighbor. Each is an opportunity to connect with a person with concerns in this life. And as you start up a conversation and listen to someone's situation, share some of the practical ideas from this book. And as you do, the conversation can flow very naturally into asking about his or her spiritual beliefs. The Bible tells us to share the Good News. And I can't think of a more appropriate time to do so.

And finally, my book should give you a sense of hope.

More than anything, I believe these ideas will give a sense of hope to those who read this book. I've heard *New York Times* best-selling author and speaker, Joyce Meyer, on her 2011 TV show, *Enjoying Everyday Life*, define it this way: "Hope is the happy anticipation that something good is going to happen."

National certified career counselors, Kevin and Kay Marie Brennfleck, say that "without hope, we lose momentum, and stop taking action to move forward. With hope, however, we are motivated to keep going. Hope enables us to believe that things *will* get better and that we *will* be able to overcome the present difficulties."[4]

So now that you have this information, I encourage you to review each entry and begin to apply it to your life. Hope is right at your fingertips.

Acknowledgements

I thank God for bringing me this great project. It was a real adventure and wonderful blessing all at the same time!

One of the first individuals that I met and worked with on the book was Jim Cermak, the chief idea guy at his marketing firm of the same name. Thank you for your always positive attitude, wonderful giving spirit, and the handful of ideas you always shared every time we met! You gave me a lot of your time and helped me so much. To Michelle Birtasevic, Amy Szabo, Roberta Schueler, and Lynn Savron, thank you for your editing help and review of the text. Special thanks to Jill Riga for all your time and expertise doing the final edit and formatting. Thanks to Brian Mowry and Jim Johnson, two fun and extremely talented guys who worked on my photos and website. Thank you Chris Roberts for your patience and perfect visual touch. Using color and creativity "Fresh Hope … Cleveland" came alive. Thanks for the great cover! I love the open door – that's exactly what hope creates!

I would also like to thank everyone from Cuyahoga Valley Church who reached out in countless ways to help me throughout this three-year journey. Great thanks to Ryan Edlind, Rick Duncan, Chad Allen, Dale Piscura, Walt Broadbent, Eric and Sharon Mack, Mike Pinchak, Bill Mc Gee (Grace Church) and Len Chipchak for your prayers, advice, and support. MaryAnn Nelich, Rosa Pozar, Christine Kowalski, Donna Mae Meyer (Grace Church), Nadeah Bikawi, and Judy Suazo, thank you for your prayers and all the odds and ends you took off my plate so that I could move forward every day with this project. I can't thank you enough for the countless things you all did to help me. Greg Jackson you were so wonderful to help with Emma, my website, and Facebook book page. And to think, it all started with a mouse! Ha Ha! Special thanks of appreciation to Bette Kala for her unselfish efforts and a big thank you also to the lovely and caring Winteregg ladies for their help. Taylor, Emma is a sweet little masterpiece. Thank you for her – she sends you a hug from every book printed.

Thanks also to the many job search groups at several local churches that provided me with accurate information for this text. I also want to thank the several pastors who read this book and shared their thoughts before it was published. I pray that the text reaches out to help members of your congregation who are struggling due to this economy. Thank you also for allowing me to incorporate your churches' information here. Your help and interest in this project was greatly appreciated. A million thanks also to the six individuals of the focus group study I conducted. They reviewed the book in August 2009. Thanks for your insight and honest evaluation of the book. Because of your efforts along with the help of Jeanne King, this book is *Fresh Hope… Cleveland*, and not *Recipes for Living in Challenging Times*. Thank you Jeanne for your help with the title! And finally, blessings to the Christian Broadcasting Network staff for their prayers each time I called! To God Be the Glory!

Author's Note

In this book, you'll find that I have pulled together community resources and wellness strategies that I acquired and practiced recently during some very difficult times in my own life. Beside what you find in this book, I also want to remind you that people can be of great help to you. They are great resources, for they can provide information, direction, and support for you as well.

To help you get the most out of this book, I have created "*Workspace*" areas. In these areas you can record other helpful ideas for your life. Each "*Workspace*" has specific directions to guide you and help you know what to record. And of course, you can always use any of the workspace areas to record anything else that you'd like including your thoughts, feelings, goals, or dreams.

When you apply the information contained in this book to your life, you and your family will gain momentum in tackling your concerns. This will also bring a sense of peace and balance to your life. In a sense, it will help you live differently. In other words, from now on you'll do things differently, and you'll leave behind some of the old habits and practices that served you so well up until now. That means how you live now will be considered the "new normal" for your life.

Change forced upon you even during a crisis can help you grow stronger and help you find a healthier way to live physically, mentally, intellectually, and spiritually. As all of us know, change is never easy. However, if you embrace change rather than fight its presence, you will be blessed in many ways. Something today that seems so difficult and overwhelming may very well be bringing you to a very lush and healthy place, a better place in your life. So welcome this time however it's unfolding for you right now. It's here for a reason.

And finally, my advice to you is simple. Don't be afraid to try something new or explore new ways to live your life. Innovative ideas can change the quality of your life, making it much more rewarding than it was before. It's possible too that you will discover things that bring healing and joy. As a breast cancer survivor, I can tell you I've tackled a few issues. And I know that good things don't always come wrapped in beautiful packages tied with gorgeous bows. Many times good things come to you through pain, struggle, and a determined spirit. So, if you are struggling today, don't give up. God is still at work in your life, even if you can't yet see the outcome your circumstances will eventually produce.

~~~~~~

<u>Important Note</u>: Please read the disclaimers on the following page. The economy could at any time change the availabilities of the services and resources you find within the pages of this book.

Disclaimers

PLEASE NOTE: Please read the following disclaimers regarding the information contained in this text.

~~~~~~

DISCLAIMER #1:

Some of the information contained in the pages of this book is of a timely nature. With the economy bringing about daily changes in some cases, you may want to verify the details of a service or agency before using it.

DISCLAIMER #2:

This information is not intended to be a replacement for the power of God's Word in your life; neither will everyone be helped by this information.

It is not meant to be a replacement for God's guidance, any type of counseling, or sound medical advice.

DISCLAIMER #3:

The author was not endorsed by any organization, service, or business listed in this book.

Creative Living Ideas

to help s-t-r-e-t-c-h your shopping dollars and other
community resources to help meet your needs

A bargain ain't a bargain
unless it's something you need.

–Sidney Carroll, television screenwriter (1913 – 1988)[5]

General Shopping Information

Thrift is as much about changing your mindset and the
way you think about all resources as it is about changing
your actions. – *S. W. Straus*[6]

~~~~~~

Some obvious ways to help make your money go further are shopping at the dollar
store, checking ads for items on sale, clipping coupons, buying items when free gifts
are offered with merchandise, and shopping sales after holidays or at the end of the
season. It's probably a good idea too, to leave your children at home while you shop.
Otherwise, you'll buy things your budget and you don't really need.

However, the very first thing you should do is seek God's wisdom, guidance and favor.
Your shopping and decision-making should always begin with prayer. Taking time
to pray will give you a moment to pause, and then you can intentionally make well-
informed decisions with God's help. It will also help you be more conscious of your
shopping behavior. Here are a few more ideas to keep in mind as well:

1. Make a budget and stick to it!

2. Make a list before you go to the store, and buy just the items on the list!

3. Coordinate your errands and stops. You'll save gas and precious time.

4. Use all clothing, food, or household items people give you if possible; get rid
   of whatever you are not using.

   Give unused items from your home to the needy, to others at your church, or
   to neighbors. Clean out cupboards and closets. Have a garage sale if possible.
   If you haven't worn clothing or used appliances in a year or more, get rid of
   them.

5. Jeff Yeager, author of *The Ultimate Cheapskate's Road to True Riches*, says,
   "Wait one week. And if you still find you need it, then get it!"[7]

6. Use this as a rule of thumb:

If you need something and money is tight, BUY JUST ONE! Need socks? Buy one package. Need pajamas? Buy just one pair. Need a few shirts? Buy just one shirt. When you only buy one, this way your needs have been met to some degree and you won't feel like you can't have anything at all. But at the same time, it will also give you peace of mind because you didn't spend a lot of money. And that will be important when the bill comes in the mail or online. Perhaps on some other day, you'll find something so very wonderful that you'll be glad God had you wait for just the right thing. But for now, buy only one.

7. Think recycling.

Before you throw something out, ask yourself, "Can I use this for something else?" For example, Gerber baby food comes in small, plastic containers. Decorate the lids, and they are perfect for holding candy, paper clips, and sugar packets. You could even put colorful stickers on the lid, line the inside, and add a sweet little note for someone on Christmas or another occasion. If you can find another use for an item, don't throw it out. If you are not sure, keep just a few.

8. Shop for items at dollar stores.

You can get wonderful wrapping paper, gift bags, party supplies, artificial flowers, and seasonal items at these discount stores.

9. Check your cupboards and closets before you shop.

A quick peek around your home to survey your family's inventory of food, clothing, and supplies will help you make wise shopping decisions.

10. Cut and use coupons, and buy only items on sale.

Better yet, use your coupons along with advertised store sales for double savings. Sit down before shopping, read through the store's weekly sales flyer, and then plan your meals around the store specials.

~ *Workspace:* Record Budget and Spending Here
What are your financial boundaries?

Financial boundaries give you guidelines so you can better live within your means. For your budget's sake, this may mean limiting purchases, gifts, holiday spending, or how often you enjoy take-out or eating at restaurants during the month.

Record your responses in Roman numeral I. For Roman numerals II and III, circle any ideas you are interested in pursuing or add your own.

~~~~~~

I. *Services or specialty items to limit or do without:*

II. *Learn to say "no" more often to the following:*

- My kids or other family members requests
- Kids coming to the grocery store when adult family members shop
- The pressure to keep up with the neighbors or what others at church seem to have
- Using credit cards ~ Instead, pay off the balances and get rid of them

III. Tune in to these:

- Listen to God more often
- Begin to develop or use your gifts and talents
- Practice "less is more" philosophy

- Don't make shopping a hobby: Try to shop only when absolutely necessary
- Seek part-time or full-employment
- Take a Dave Ramsey's Financial Peace University class (www.daveramsey.com)
- Volunteer or help others in some meaningful way

Resources:
a source of supply, support, or aid,
especially that one can draw upon
when needed.

–Dictionary.com

Services Available within the Community

*F*resh ideas for your life begin here! Take a look at these services available in the community, along with other creative ideas for your life. Be open-minded and consider all things to be helpful in this directory. If something doesn't pertain to your situation, gently toss it aside and move on.

All services here are listed alphabetically. At the end of this section, there is a place where you can record information that you discover to help make your life even better.

~~~~~~

BEAUTY / GROOMING

A new haircut will make you feel like a million bucks. But you don't have to spend a fortune to look great. At most of the salons listed here, a haircut will cost you about the same as a meal at your favorite fast food restaurant. Quite a deal! You'll find additional information for each facility in Appendix B.

1. Cuyahoga Valley Career Center (Brecksville)
   - A variety of services are offered by appointment, including all chemical services, up-dos, coloring, facials, manicures, pedicures, and waxing.

2. Grace College of Cosmetology (Middleburg Heights)
   - Walk-in appointments only.
   - All hair services are offered, facial waxing/tweezing, and natural nail manicures. For hair relaxing, call ahead.*

3. Cisoria Academy of Cosmetology (Maple Heights)
   - Walk-in appointments only.

4. The Cut Beauty School (Cleveland Heights)
   - All hair services are offered.*

BEAUTY / GROOMING *(continued)*

5. Fairview Academy O & D Beauty, Inc. (Fairview Park)

    - All hair services are offered, plus manicures, pedicures, facials, and facial waxing.*
    - Haircuts, perms, color, and relaxing are all offered at great prices.

6. Inner State Beauty School (Lyndhurst)

    - Schedule these services two weeks in advance: manicures, pedicures, waxing, and facials.
    - All hair services are offered, plus manicures, pedicures, facials and facial waxing.*
    - Daily specials on services and senior citizens' discount.

7. Lake Erie Barber College (Cleveland)

    - Walk-ins accepted.
    - Senior citizens' discount on some services.
    - Services offered: cuts, color, body waves, perms and relaxers.

8. Paul Mitchell – The Ohio Academy (Twinsburg)

    - Walk-ins are accepted. Appointment required for perms or relaxers.
    - Most hair services are offered including: color, highlights, styles, updo's, block coloring, perms, and relaxers. Manicures done, but not acrylics.

9. Normandy Cosmetology Clinic (Parma)

    - Walk-ins are accepted.
    - Services offered include: haircuts, perms, relaxers, and color; bring your own.
    - All hair services are offered, as well as braiding, manicures, facials and facial waxing.

10. Polaris's New Beginnings Salon, *inside Polaris Career Center* (Middleburg Heights)

    - Appointments are required for all services.
    - Services offered include: haircuts, color, and nail services.

11. Raphael's School of Beauty (North Olmsted)

    - Walk-ins are accepted depending on student availability.
    - All hair services are offered including: haircuts, braiding, manicures, pedicures, facials, and facial waxing.*

*All hair services = cuts, highlights, perms, body waves, chemical relaxers, & up-do's.

BUSINESS / BUDGETING

The office genie has granted you three wishes. Use the tips below to make your wishes of saving money, obtaining free business cards, and having money flow toward you...all come true!

1. Cut larger Post-It® notes in half to make them go further.

2. Use both the front and back sides of your laser jet, ink jet, or copier papers. Don't throw away paper if the other side can be used for printing document drafts, projects, or lists.

3. Visit www.vistaprint.com for free business cards. All you pay is shipping.

4. Consider getting the monthly closing dates for your Visa, MasterCard, and other major credit cards. Knowing these dates can help you plan your purchases. That's because charges after the closing dates will appear on the following month's bill. Call customer service for your accounts' closing dates through the end of the year.

CAR INSURANCE OPTIONS

Fred Flintstone may not have had it. However, here are some car insurance options for your jalopy.

1. Have your car insurance (renter's and home owner's too) deducted monthly from your checking account. Paying your insurance this way is a good way to eliminate panic or scrambling to pay the full six-month premium when it's due.

   And while this approach will not save you money in the long run, you will benefit most from the peace of mind this option offers. That's because it helps you manage your expenses in a very wise and practical way perhaps at a time when you need it most. A small monthly administrative fee of about $1.00 will apply. Call your insurance agent for details.

2. Consider increasing your deductibles to lower your rates.

DENTAL SERVICES ~ *You don't want to lose your choppers!*

1. For help with non-covered, non-emergency dental services, contact Ohio Dental Options, at 1-888-765-6789. To see if you qualify, fill out an application and submit it with financial and other required information. You can print out an application from their website, and fax it to: (216) 676-1323, ATTN: Dental Options.

2. For other dental services, contact the Case School of Dental Medicine at (216) 368-8730, the Free Clinic at (216) 721-4010 or Normandy High School of Dental Technologies in Parma (September – May only) at (440) 843-1383. At Case School of Dental Medicine, there is a non-refundable $80 fee for x-rays and an exam to initiate a patient record. No personal checks are accepted.

3. Negotiate lower fees with your dentist before you receive services. His/her patient load may be suffering due to the economy. You never know until you ask.

4. Remit Payment. Ask to send in your payment at a later date.

5. If you do not have the money to visit the dentist, at least brush and floss several times a day. Hold your toothbrush at a 45° angle and brush from the very top of the tooth just under the gum line. This will remove plaque and prevent decay. Medical experts say flossing your teeth each day will add one to two years to your life!

EATING OUT

A change of scenery and your favorite dish can make the world look so much better! Not sure if you can afford your favorite eatery? Try a selection or two from the menu below, and see what works for you.

1. Pack your lunch. The experts say you will not only save about $1,200 a year, but you will eat healthier as well.

2. Don't order a beverage when eating out. Drink water. Because water is usually free at most restaurants, you can shave several dollars off your bill if you

Eating Out *(continued)*

forego coffee and soft drinks. This will be especially helpful when dining out as a family. However, nutritionists advocate that diet soft drinks are terrible for you. The artificial sweeteners in them can trigger diabetes and weight gain by making your body actually crave more sugar. And the sodium and calories you'll consume in regular carbonated beverages are equally harmful.

3. If you are out shopping or doing errands during the day, take along a healthy snack with you instead of stopping for fast food. Packing your lunch and thinking ahead will save you money, calories, and you will eat healthier. Pack fruit, granola bars, muffins, and sandwiches like peanut butter and jelly that will keep without refrigeration. Stop at the park if it's nearby and enjoy your goodies. *Bon appétit!*

EMPLOYMENT INFORMATION / CAREER SEMINARS

Success in life depends on your ability to persevere.

1. The Cuyahoga Valley Career Center in Brecksville offers free career development seminars through the year. Contact the Program Developer, Patricia Coyne, at (440) 746-8233.

2. Career seminars, computer training classes, and help with your job search are all offered at the Employment Connection. Classes are free. To schedule an orientation session for the Parma location, call (216) 898-1366. See their website at www.employmentconnection.us for more Cuyahoga County offices and other Ohio county locations.

3. Need to use a computer? All branches of the Cuyahoga County Public Library system have computers available for patrons' use. Use your library card or library guest pass to log in. Computers are available on a first-come, first-serve basis. The Internet and other programs are available.

4. Mimi Vanderhaven's newspaper allows you to place a free "Clever Classified" ad in the Employment, For Sale, Professional Services, and other sections (circulation in Cuyahoga, Medina, and Summit counties). Log on to the website at www.mimiave.com/cleverclassifieds/ to create your account.

EMPLOYMENT INFORMATION / CAREER SEMINARS *(continued)*

5. Put all your qualifications on LinkedIn.com, one of the social media. It's perfect for finding career and consulting opportunities, business deals, and more! Go to www.LinkedIn.com to create your profile.

6. If you need help with career issues and ideas for job opportunities that utilize your skills and gifts, check out the Christian book, *Live Your Calling: A Practical Guide to Finding & Fulfilling Your Mission in Life.* Authors Kevin and Kay Marie Brennfleck are national certified career counselors.

7. Check out www.christiancareercenter.com to view new jobs, articles on job hunting, tips for today's economy, and more. "What's Your Excuse?", an article in a February 2009 issue, discusses how we can partner with God in our challenges by taking charge of our attitude.[8]

8. In a career transition? Perform a SWOT (strengths, weaknesses, opportunities, and threats) analysis to identify your career goals. Then do a gap analysis – the gaps between the skills, training, and experience you have and those you need to get the job you want (per Career Developer, Patricia Coyne at the Cuyahoga Valley Career Center).[9]

9. The biggest challenge for many job seekers – especially ones who have been dropped into the world of unemployment without warning – is time management. Paul Meshanko, time-management specialist and managing partner for the Edge Learning Institute of Ohio, recommends creating a designated work space. "Go to Panera with a laptop, or Borders. This takes you out of your private-time environment." Creating a daily game plan is also important. "Sit down with your first cup of coffee and prioritize the day's activities," Menshanko says. "Focus on end results. Which tasks do you need to do today and which tasks can wait until tomorrow?" (Learning to Manage Time, Pflaum).[10]

10. So that you're not tempted to ramble on about your story in a job interview, sit down before the meeting and identify two things about yourself that are relevant to the position. This is not only a good strategy, but it also allows the interviewer to develop follow-up questions about your experience ("Your Job Hunt," Stringer).[11]

EMPLOYMENT INFORMATION / CAREER SEMINARS *(continued)*

11. Below are some local job search groups. Some phone numbers listed below are for the contact person – not the church. See Appendix C for contact names.

- Bay United Methodist Church in Bay Village (Job Seekers): (440) 871-2082
- Fairmount Presbyterian Church in Cleveland Heights: (216) 321-5800
- Grace Church in Middleburg Heights: (440) 243-4885
- Parkside Church in Bainbridge/Solon: (440) 543-1212
- Pioneer Memorial Presbyterian Church /Solon: (440) 248-4756 (Chagrin Valley Job Seekers Group)
- St. Albert the Great Catholic Church in North Royalton: (440) 237-6760
- St. Basil Catholic Church in Brecksville: (440) 526-1686
- St. Paul's Episcopal Church in Cleveland Heights: (216) 932-5815

FOOD / FOOD STORAGE

My chrome wagon is always filled with organic salad greens and fresh fruit. You ARE what you eat!

1. Never go to the grocery store hungry. And if at all possible, try not to take your young children with you as well. Both situations may affect the purchases you make. And you will most likely spend more money, defeating your very purpose.

2. Buy store-brand items at the grocery store, which are cheaper and are just as good. Store brands are especially good in dishes like stews and soups, where the appearance doesn't need to be that spectacular. If you are garnishing a desert, for example, you will probably want to use fresh, not canned. Giant Eagle and ValueTime brands are fine for many purposes. However, if you are not certain you will like the product, buy what you usually do so that you won't waste your money.

3. Use dried herbs instead of fresh. Fresh herbs have wonderful flavor and aroma, but they spoil quickly. On the other hand, dried herbs can last for months in your pantry.

4. Did you know that you can freeze butter? Take advantage of sale prices and try it for holiday baking or simply stock up for future needs.

FOOD / FOOD STORAGE *(continued)*

5. Freeze leftover pasta sauce, applesauce, and unused portions of milk or soy milk in glass bottles. You may find you simply cannot eat or drink some of your food items before they spoil or the expiration date passes. Freezing prevents waste and certainly gives you peace of mind, because you will know you didn't waste your money!

   Note: Freeze or microwave all food items and water in glass. Never use plastic wrap or plastic dishes. The process of heating or freezing in plastic releases chemical compounds into your food or beverage that have been linked to cancer.

6. **Cheap sources of protein include:** kidney beans, any dried beans or lentils, and natural peanut butter which contains only peanuts and salt. These are all good sources of vegetable protein.

   Because our bodies do not manufacture protein, children and adults need it every day. Health care professionals suggest a diet rich in mostly vegetable proteins, along with lean poultry and fish. Watch the amount of red meat you eat.

   NOTE: Stay away from peanut butter brands that are not natural, because they may contain sugar and/or hydrogenated oils.

7. Shop at bakery thrift shops. Buy bread, bagels, cakes, and cookies at a third the price of your local grocery store. Although items are sold close to their expiration date, they are still good. Freeze them to extend their shelf life. Entenmann's are located in Strongsville and Lyndhurst. Schwebel's Shops are in Cleveland, Euclid, and Strongsville. Find Wonder/Hostess Shops in Parma Heights. Prices are cheaper than Wal-Mart. See Appendix D for complete address information for all locations.

   NOTE: Select items that do not contain high fructose corn syrup or hydrogenated oils. High fructose corn syrup produces a craving in the body for more sugar, and too much sugar can ultimately lead to diabetes. Hydrogenated oils, on the other hand, clog arteries, possibly leading to stroke or heart attack over time.

FOOD / FOOD STORAGE *(continued)*

8. Aldi grocery stores have many good deals. Bring your own paper bags (or pay for theirs) and deposit a 25¢ refundable grocery cart fee. Read your labels carefully. They sell economical paper products and produce. No-frills shopping there means no organic or brand-name items. All Aldi stores accept the Ohio Direction Card food stamp voucher program.

9. Sign up to receive e-mails from Heinen's on their weekly specials and recipes at: www.heinens.com. Click the Tasteful Rewards tab. You will need your Heinen's Preferred Customer Card to begin the process.

▪ **FOOD SHOPPING / FOOD STAMP PROGRAM** ▪ *(public assistance)*

The Ohio Direction Card (food stamp voucher program) *is accepted* at these stores:
- Aldi
- Entenmann's Bakery Stores
- Giant Eagle
- Heinen's
- Marc's
- Wal-Mart

GIVE, RECEIVE, OR BARTER ~ *creative ways to get what you need*

1. Faith Classifieds is a place to not only barter with other Christians (share your skills and receive other services), but you can also buy, sell, or trade on a website that is Christian-owned and operated. Everything is free, but there is a limit of ten ads posted per month per person. Each ad expires in thirty days. Go to www.faithclassifieds.com.

2. The Freecycle Network, a grassroots and entirely non-profit movement, lets people give (and receive) things for free in their own towns, thus keeping good things out of landfills. Membership is free, and everything posted must be free, legal, and appropriate for all ages. To view the items being given away and/or items sought, you must be a member of the local group. Go to www.freecycle.org and sign up with the group nearest you.

AT HOME

Home is the place where it feels right to walk around without shoes.

– Author unknown[12]

1. If your bathroom has a lot of lights, buy a night-light to save electricity. You'd be surprised at how much you can actually do using only a night-light. And if you are looking for a more enchanting experience, light candles in your bathroom and enjoy their glow as you freshen up.

2. Make your holiday and birthday cards. Card stock can be bought very inexpensively. This could be a great family project. Purchase card stock and other art supplies at Hollos Papercraft, 1878 Pearl Road, Brunswick (past Route 303). Low prices and a large selection of art supplies will make the drive well worth your time and gas!

3. Use clean dish towels to dry vegetables and salad greens. Towels can be washed and used over and over again. This will help you use fewer paper towels and save our trees as well. Purchase several of them at Marc's or the dollar store.

4. Make your own cloth napkins and use these instead of paper napkins. Cloth napkins can be used again and again, and all you have to do is add them to your regular wash. If you don't have a sewing machine to hem the edges, use pinking shears to keep them from raveling. Check the markdown fabric table at Jo-Ann Fabrics. Add some color to your dining table by mixing and matching several different print and colored fabrics.

More ~ Practical ideas that can s-t-r-e-t-c-h your dollars!

5. Wash used plastic bags, storage bags, and other ziplock bags. DO NOT reuse plastic storage bags used for meat, cheese, and veggies. Reusing these could spread harmful bacteria.

6. Cut your fabric softener dryer sheets in half or thirds to s-t-r-e-t-c-h your dollars.

AT HOME *(continued)*

7. Using plain white, store-brand paper towels instead of fancy decorated ones will stretch your dollars. Enjoy saving as much as sixty cents or more a roll.

8. Mix the last of the shampoo left in the bottle with a little water – use it!

9. Use microfiber cloths (those made of polyester and polyamide) to clean mirrors, glass, and eyeglasses. These miracle cloths are fabulous, especially because you don't need to use any cleaning solution! Just spray or sprinkle the mirror or glass item (table, picture frame, etc.) with a little water and let the environmentally-friendly cloth go to work! Find Micro Fiber™ Miracle Cloths at Marc's and select local supermarkets.

▪ HEALTH CLUB MEMBERSHIP ▪

Healthy options for you!

1. If it's time to renew your gym membership, keep in mind that your health club may allow you to purchase a restricted membership. A restricted membership would allow you to use the facilities for two to three days a week. Call customer service for help or get the phone number of the district supervisor, who can process your request. Restricted memberships are usually about 50 percent cheaper.

2. Become a mall walker, it won't cost you a dime! Most malls' main entrances open about 9:00 a.m. And without the crowds of shoppers, it's a perfect time to put on your walking shoes and join other folks in their quest for health and fitness. Call your local mall office for more details.

3. If you can't afford a gym membership, try starting your own fitness class with friends and neighbors. Pick some cool music, get a hula hoop, and add a few weights. And of course, you can always go to the park to walk or walk in your neighborhood as well. Walking is one of the best things you can do for your body and your mind. All you need is a pair of walking shoes and 30 minutes of your time.

▪ HOME HEATING ASSISTANCE (HEAP) ▪

This program will help keep your tootsies warm!

The Home Energy Assistance Program (HEAP) can help with your home heating bill. Apply in early August for the coming winter season. The application will ask for employment and financial information. Contact the Ohio Department of Development at 1-800-282-0880 or online at www.energy.ohio.gov.

MEDICAL INFORMATION

- Listen to your body. What it's telling you is important.

- Men: You neglect medical issues more than anyone on the planet. You rationalize away symptoms. But, caught early, many illnesses are treatable, with a good prognosis.

- Be smart; don't let a medical issue go untreated because you think you cannot afford it.

- On the next page, you will find medical services in your community that will be like a warm hug right when you need it!

1. **Medication:** If possible, ask your doctor for medication samples.

2. **Medical Services:** MetroHealth Medical Center will rate you financially and discount many health care services. To see if you qualify, call any satellite location. Each specialty area at the main campus will also rate you for services (cancer care, orthopedics, emergency, etc.). To make an appointment with the financial counselor at the Strongsville campus at 16000 Pearl Rd., Suite 309, call (440) 238-2124. Because so many folks need assistance these days, you may have to wait a month or more for an appointment.

3. **Medical Services for Uninsured:** Providers of Health Care Services
   - Care Alliance: 1530 St. Clair Avenue – Cleveland; (216) 781-6724
   - Free Clinic of Greater Cleveland: 12201 Euclid Avenue – Cleveland; (216) 721-4010

MEDICAL INFORMATION *(continued)*

- Neighborhood Family Practice: 3569 Ridge Rd. – Cleveland; (216) 281-0872
- North Coast Health Ministry *(serves western Cuyahoga & Lorain counties)*: 16110 Detroit Avenue – Lakewood; (216) 228-7878
- Parma Health Ministry: Parma Community General Hospital *(serves Parma, Parma Heights, North Royalton, Seven Hills)*: 7007 Powers Blvd. – Parma; (440) 843-8087
- Southwest General Neighborhood Care Center *(serves Berea, Brookpark, Columbia, Columbia Township, Middleburg Heights, Olmsted Falls, & Strongsville)*: 17951 Jefferson Park Drive, Middleburg Heights; (440) 816-6444.
- Medina Health Ministry: 425 W. Liberty St., Suite 1, Medina; (330) 764-9300
- Lorain County Free Clinic: 3323 Pearl Avenue -- Lorain; (440) 277-7602
- Lorain County Health & Dentistry: 1800 Livingston Avenue, Lorain; (440) 233-0166
- Lake County Free Clinic *(serves Ashtabula, Geauga, & Lake counties)*: 54 South State Street, Room 302 -- Painesville

MEDICARE

Tony Bennett might fly you to the moon, but when you come back down to earth, this information may be helpful too!

1. Apply for *regular* Medicare benefits three months before your sixty-fifth birthday, and up until three months after your sixty-fifth birthday. This does not apply to disability or end-stage renal disease. Have your Social Security number available. For more information, call Medicare at 1-800-633-4227.

2. Between October 15 through December 7, anyone can join, switch, or drop a Medicare prescription drug plan – Medicare Part D. For more information, call Medicare at 1-800-633-4227 or visit them at www.medicare.gov. You can also enroll on the plan's website or call the plan directly to enroll.

Medical Inventory: Record the last time you received the services below if appropriate. If you haven't had these tests done recently, make an appointment with your doctor or dentist today.

I. Men (ages 45 /50): PSA Blood Test (screening for prostate cancer)
    Women: Mammogram / breast self-exam / PAP smear

II. Blood Tests and More

    - Blood Pressure
    - Cholesterol
    - Glucose blood Sugar Level
    - Complete Blood Count
    - Vitamin D Level
    - Calcium (osteoporosis)

III. Colonoscopy (age 50)

    Depression Screening

IV. Dental Exam (every 6 months)

    Hearing / Vision Tests

V. Shots

    - Flu Shot (every October)
    - Pneumonia Shot
    - Tetanus Shot (every 10 years)
    - Allergy Shot

VI. Report problems ~ Do you need prescription refills?

    - Swelling, bruising, bleeding, headache, dizziness, shortest of breath, mass or lump, pain
    - Weight Gain / Loss
    - Medication Refills / Inhaler

Workspace: Record Medical Information
~ What Are Your Symptoms: Body, Appetite, Mood? ~

Record Your Symptoms: Keep track of changes in your body, appetite, or mood. Record below any symptoms you've noticed lately. Remember to record the date they caught your attention too. This will help your physician know how to treat you.

Record Other Changes Here: Changes to your medication, diet, vitamins, exercise, strength, and sleep hygiene can affect your health as well. Record those changes here.

Praise the Lord; may I never forget the good things He does for me. He forgives all my sins and heals all my diseases. –The Living Bible (Psalm 103: 2- 3)

MORTGAGE INFORMATION

A house is made of walls and beams; a home is built with love and dreams. – *Author unknown*[13]

1. Save the Dream, the State of Ohio's new foreclosure prevention program, provides information for those concerned about paying their mortgage.

   Ph: 1-(888) 404-4674

   Website: www.savethedream.ohio.gov

2. The Cuyahoga County Treasurer and the Cuyahoga Court of Common Pleas have developed these nationally recognized programs to help you.

   Ohio Housing Finance Agency
   http://www.ohiohome.org/

   Cuyahoga County Foreclosure Prevention Program
   http://www.dontborrowtroublecc.org/

   Neighborhood Housing Services of Greater Cleveland
   http://www.nhscleveland.org/programs/CuyahogaCountyForeclosureProgram.htm

   Cuyahoga County Foreclosure Mediation Program
   http://cp.cuyahogacounty.us/internet/ForeClosureMediation.aspx
   http://cp.cuyahogacounty.us/internet/CourtDocs%5CForeclosureMediation.pdf

SOCIAL SERVICE AGENCIES

Long ago, there was a little field mouse named Emma. Her job at the factory was slow and her cupboards were almost bare. But most of all, Emma was very sad because she had no cheese. Still, she knew God would provide for her needs. So each night she lit a candle and prayed. Then one evening, a knock at her door brought an amazing answer to her prayers.

And, like Emma, the agencies on the next page may be an answer to your prayers.

LOCAL SOCIAL SERVICE AGENCIES AND COMMUNITY SUPPORTS

1. *FIRST CALL FOR HELP* is United Way's special service to help those in need twenty-four hours a day. Simply call *2-1-1* to access help in Cuyahoga, Geauga, and Medina Counties (Website: http://211cleveland.org). Have your pen and paper ready so that they can direct you to local food banks, rent assistance programs, medical services, counseling, legal services, unemployment offices, and many more agencies that will provide help to you and/or your family. Depending on the volume of incoming calls, it may take ten to twenty minutes before an information specialist is able to help you.

2. **Lutheran Family Services (LFS)** is a faith-based not-for-profit community agency. They provide domestic and international adoption, mental health counseling, pregnancy counseling, and power parenting. They also help students and families grow healthy and strong through both school and community outreach programs. These programs help deal with abuse, violence, anger management, depression, and marital and family issues. (See next page).

   Although their name suggests a connection with the Lutheran Church, you don't need to be Lutheran to take advantage of their services. Office locations include: Brooklyn, Chagrin Falls, Cuyahoga Falls, Fairview Park, North Royalton, and Ohio City. For more information call (216) 281-2500 to speak with an in-take specialist. Medicaid benefits are accepted.
   Website: http://lfsohio.org

3. **Ohio Department of Jobs and Family Services** provides many programs to help you and your family. Check their website or see the government pages of your phone book to find the office near you.

   Ph: (216) 987-7000
   Website: www.jfs.ohio.gov/ohp

   Programs Include:

   - Children's Feeding Programs
   - Child Support Services
   - Disability Services
   - Emergency Assistance
   - Employment
   - Food Stamps
   - Heath Insurance (Medicaid)
   - Job Training
   - Transportation

LOCAL SOCIAL SERVICE AGENCIES AND COMMUNITY SUPPORTS *(continued)*

4. **Social Worker (Hospital):** The hospital's social worker knows illness can bring social, emotional, and financial concerns. A medical social worker can refer you directly to agencies and programs in the community for assistance. Whether you are the patient, a friend, or a family member of the patient, you do not need a doctor's referral to take advantage of these services.

TAX SERVICES & CREDIT / FICO REPORT INFORMATION

Free help with taxes and you don't have to be fifty! Now that's living!

1. The American Association of Retired Persons (AARP) will do your taxes for free! Amazingly enough, you don't need to be a senior citizen or an AARP member to take advantage of this service. Taxes are prepared February through April. Appointments are taken beginning early January. Call AARP at 1-888-OUR-AARP (1-(888) 687-2277), or go to www.aarp.org. They may not be able to handle all income tax issues.

    Note: There are great deals *available* on cars and houses because of the economy. To make sure your wishes can come true, check your credit information now to ensure that there is nothing to keep you from purchasing any large-ticket items in the future.

    It is also good to make sure that you haven't unknowingly become a victim of credit fraud and/or identity theft.

2. Credit reports can be obtained by contacting the three credit reporting agencies:

    1) Equifax: 1-800-525-6285
    www.equifax.com; P.O. Box 740241, Atlanta, GA 30374-0241

    2) Experian: 1-888-397-3742
    www.experian.com; P.O. Box 9532, Allen, TX 75013-9532

    3) TransUnion: 1-800-680-7289
    www.transunion.com; P.O. Box 6790, Fullerton, CA 92834-6790

TAX SERVICES & CREDIT / FICO REPORT INFORMATION *(continued)*

4) For a free FICO report and more information also check www.myfico.com. FICO scores (credit score) will provide you with both a number score (0-850) and a grade range (from *A-F*), and also show you how your credit scores compare to other individuals in the nation.

WARDROBE / SHOPPING

Looking your best doesn't necessarily have to take a lot of cash.

1. Goodwill operates several resale stores. Find good deals on the east side at: 2295 E. 55th Street, Ph: (216) 431-8300; and 2720 Van Aken Blvd., Ph: (216) 295-5684 locations. Go north and find bargains at Goodwill's North Olmsted location, 23100 Lorain Avenue, Ph: (440) 777-4422. On the southeast side of town, shop at 12650 Rockside Road, Garfield Heights, Ph: (440) 581-6320. And finally, heading east, shop at the Eastlake location: 33459 Vine Street, Ph:(440) 942-6910.

2. Shop at the Salvation Army stores for used clothing and appliances. There is a large Salvation Army store at 8623 Pearl Road, Middleburg Heights (near Wal-Mart). Wednesday is sale day, with items sold at up to 50 percent off. Be prepared to hunt through the racks.

3. Betty's Boutique is a friendly, confidential store at Willoughby Hills Friends Church where individuals in need can come to "shop" for free. The boutique is north of Cuyahoga County, give them a call at (440) 944-1026 or visit them on the Web at http://www.whfriends.org/pages/outreach.shtml.

4. Check out Curvy Consignments at 13902 Puritas Avenue, Cleveland. They specialize in plus sizes. Open Friday-Sunday. Ph: (216) 251-9591.

5. Shop at resale or consignment shops. Visit the Red Geranium Consignment Shop for all types of things. They carry vintage clothing items along with collectibles, antiques, and housewares. This North Royalton shop is located at 13803 Ridge Road. Ph: (440) 237-2000.

Wardrobe / Shopping *(continued)*

A little imagination could bring forth a new you!

6. Shop at specialty consignment shops like the Wren House. Located at 31 South Franklin Street in Chagrin Falls, the Wren House carries many brand-name labels. Because this shop may be a little "out of the way," you may want to call first to find out specifically what they carry. Ph: (440) 247-6566.

7. Visit the *Restyle Resale* shop for designer, brand-name clothing. This shop is located at 10015 West 130th Street, north of Albion in North Royalton. For more information, call (440) 582-3006.

8. You'll enjoy visiting Thrift Nation, an innovative second-hand store located at 6286 Pearl Road in Parma Heights. They sell clothing, furniture, books, antiques, and everything in between. To find out more, call the store at (440) 886-3300.

9. The American Cancer Society operates two resale shops. All proceeds go to help those with cancer. Shop at Discovery Shop East: 5404 Mayfield Road, Lyndhurst. Ph: (440) 461-9034); and Discovery Shop West: 20470 Lorain Avenue, Fairview Park. Ph: (440) 333-6307.

See Appendix A for more shopping discount information. See also the business phone book online, under "Consignment Shops" and "Resale Shops." Happy bargain hunting!

Workspace: Record Other Helpful Ideas You Discover
~ Spend Less ▪ Enjoy More ~

Record Your Ideas: The section you just read gave you general shopping information, all types of services located in the community, and creative ways to meet some of your challenges. Perhaps this information brought to mind more ideas that could be of help to you and your family. Record those ideas below.

Record Ways to Change Your Spending Habits: To help you save money, you may also want to record the specific ways you'll go about changing your spending habits. For example, if you stop to buy a cup of coffee every day before work, you could save money by only stopping to buy coffee twice a week. Record your goals for saving money below. Record also the actions you will take to change your spending habits.

You can get shoes for eighty-five cents at the bowling alley. *– Author unknown*[14]

If you watch a game,

it's fun.

If you play it, it's recreation.

If you work at it, it's golf.

-Bob Hope, (1903 – 2003),
English-born American Actor, Comedian, and Clevelander [15]

Affordable Entertainment
~ find just what you're looking for ~

Cleveland offers a variety of free or very affordable activities to enjoy throughout the year. The general information below shares local publications and resources to help you.

On the next several pages, you'll find a variety of things to do in the Cleveland area including activities for the arts, exploration, festivals, recreation, tours, and just for kids.

GENERAL INFORMATION:

❖ AAA Auto Club Newsletter ~ Lists information on festivals in your community and in other parts of the country as well. Check for monthly events at: www.aaa.com.

❖ Cleveland Visitor's Guide ~ Information on Cleveland for the visitor or new resident. http://cleveland.about.com/od/visitingcleveland/ig/Cleveland-Ohio-Visitors-Guide/.

❖ Cleveland Weekly Newsletter ~ A free weekly e-mail newsletter about Cleveland. To sign up, go to: www.cleveland.about.com/gi/pages/stay.htm

❖ Community Festivals ~ Check your community's website and local newspapers for festivals right in your backyard!

❖ Cuyahoga County Public Library ~ Cleveland has one of the best library systems in the country. Beside books, you can also borrow tapes, DVDs, and CDs all for free to Cuyahoga County residents. Also available at each branch: *Library Programs*, a seasonal publication sharing information on free classes and events. For online information, go to: http://cuyahogalibrary.org/EventFinder. aspx?TodaysEvents=true.

❖ Entertainment Book ~ This book offers discounts on restaurants, sports events, movies, recreation, and many more attractions for the Greater Cleveland/ Akron area. Visit: www.entertainment.com/discount/home.shtml.

❖ New Resident's Guide to Cleveland ~ Helpful information if you are new to the area. Visit: http://cleveland.about.com/od/livingincleveland/tp/newresidentsguide. htm.

❖ Sandy's Cleveland Blog ~ All the latest information about Cleveland, posted several times a week at: http://cleveland.about.com/b/.

▪ arts ▪

Summer Events

❖ Boston Mills Art Show (end of June - July 4th weekend)
   Website: www.bmbw.com/events-and-activities/boston-mills-artfest

❖ The World-Famous Cleveland Orchestra (July)
   Free - July 4th weekend concert & fireworks held annually on Public Square.
   Website: www.clevelandorchestra.com/
   Ph: (216) 231-1111

❖ Tremont: Arts in August Series
   Lincoln Park, West 14th & Starkweather, Tremont
   The Arts in August Series exposes the people of Tremont, Greater Cleveland, and
   Cuyahoga County to the beauty and positive influence of the arts.
   Website: www.tremontwest.org/index/arts-in-august

❖ Wade Oval Wednesdays
   Free summer concert series at University Circle on Wednesdays, along with
   extended hours at the Cleveland Botanical Garden, the Cleveland Museum of
   Natural History, and the Cleveland Museum of Art.
   Website: www.universitycircle.org/uci.aspx?type=page&page=82

❖ More Events at University Circle
   Website: www.universitycircle.org

Year-Round Events

❖ Calendar of arts and cultural events in Ohio ~ it's free!
   Website: www.artsinohio.com

❖ The Cleveland Museum of Art
   11150 East Boulevard, Cleveland
   Free daily admission to the museum's permanent art collection.
   Website: www.clevelandart.org/ Ph: (216) 421-7340

❖ Parma Theatre
   5826 Ridge Road, Cleveland ~ Monday-Thursday evenings & matinees: $4.50
   Ph: (440) 885-0600

❖ Tremont ArtWalk
   Enjoy this artwalk every second Friday of the month, all year. ArtWalk map available
   on the website listed here. Website: www.tremontartwalk.org/

▪ exploration ▪

❖ Lake View Cemetery
Learn about Cleveland's history: self-guided auto tours, trolley tours, and trail guides.
Website: www.lakeviewcemetery.com

❖ The Old Arcade
(between Euclid and Superior Avenues, just off Public Square)
Opened 1890 ~ one of the first indoor shopping centers in America.
Ph: (216) 696-1408
Websites: http://theclevelandarcade.com/ and
http://theclevelandarcade.com/content/history (courtesy of About.com)

❖ Antiquing
1. Visit Larchmere Avenue (near Shaker Square). Hunt for antique glassware, china, and furniture.

   Websites:

   • Larchmere Ave.: http://cleveland.about.com/od/neighborhoods/p/shaker square.htm
   • Larchmere Ave.: www.larchmere.com/
   • Shaker Square: www.shakersquare.net/

2. Enjoy shopping on Lorain Avenue (between W. 35th and W. 45th Streets) for architectural antiques (courtesy of About.com).

❖ Take your own architectural tour of Cleveland.
Visit these sites:

   • *Rock-n-Rock Hall of Fame & Museum* (Architect: I. M. Pei)
   • *"Free" Stamp* (Designer: Claes Oldenburg)
   • *Old Arcade* (Architects: John M. Eisenmann and George H. Smith)
   • *Terminal Tower* (Designed by the firm of Graham, Anderson, Probst & White)

More information on the Terminal Tower:
http://www.clevelandseniors.com/people/terminal-tower.htm

▪ festivals ▪

Summer ~ Fall

❖ Feast of the Assumption in Little Italy (August)
An annual four-day street celebration which includes a parade, food, crafts, and music, all commemorating the Catholic Day of Assumption.
Websites:
www.cleveland.com/feast-of-the-assumption
www.littleitalycleveland.com

❖ Ingenuity Festival (September)
Free. Combines art and technology in a weekend-long celebration.
Ph: (216) 589-9444
Website: www.ingenuitycleveland.com

❖ Mapleside Farms
It will be interesting to see what the new owners have planned for this working farm and orchard. View the blog on their website for more information.
294 Pearl Road – Brunswick, Ohio 44212
Ph: (330) 225-5576
Website: www.mapleside.com

❖ Twins Day Festival (1st full weekend in August ~ Twinsburg, Ohio)
Twins from all over the U.S. come for a special weekend.
Website: www.twinsdays.org

❖ *Sweetest Day (October)*
What is Sweetest Day?
Sweetest Day is a special Cleveland holiday dating back to 1922, initially started to bring some happiness and cheer to children in orphanages, the disabled, and shut-ins. Although the intent has changed, the tradition of giving candy, flowers, and gifts continues in Cleveland. A few other cities in the Midwest also observe this holiday. Clevelanders observe Sweetest Day the third Saturday in October.

▪ festivals ▪

Christmas ~ Winter

❖ *Country Lights* (December)
Enjoy Christmas lights in the country when you visit Lake Farm Park, a working farm and education center located in Kirtland, Ohio -- just a short drive from Cleveland.
Website: www.lakemetroparks.com

❖ Rockefeller Park Greenhouse (December)
Enjoy seeing beautiful holiday plants including poinsettias. The greenhouse is located near University Circle. Admission is free.
Website: www.rockefellergreenhouse.org/

❖ *WinterFest Holiday Lighting* (November)
This is an annual Cleveland event the Saturday evening after Thanksgiving! Grab your coat and scarf and help kick off the holiday season, complete with tree lighting and fireworks on Cleveland's Public Square.
Blog: www.ohiofestivals.net

❖ The Cleveland Home & Garden Show (January)
Here you will find celebrity gardens, gardening demonstrations, dozens of gardening and home improvement vendors, and food and beverages. The show was moved to the Great Lakes Expo Center in Euclid, Ohio in 2010.
Website: www.homeandflower.com/cleveland/

❖ The Greater Cleveland Auto Show (February - March)
This annual event is held at the I-X Center and features production, classic, and the latest concept vehicles. The Auto Show lasts for about ten days.
Website: www.clevelandautoshow.com

❖ Medina Ice Festival (February)
Free ice-carving festival and contest in Medina, 33 miles south of Cleveland.
Website: www.medinacountyevents.com

❖ Punderson State Park's Great Dog Sled Race (January)
Free to spectators ~ Punderson State Park is 30 miles east of Cleveland in Geauga County on Route 87.
Website: www.friendsofpunderson.com

▪ festivals ▪

Winter ~ Spring

❖ St. Patrick's Day Parade (March 17)
   The St. Patrick's Day parade has been a Cleveland tradition since 1867. View the parade from any place along Euclid Avenue. After the parade, go for corned beef and cabbage at one of the local restaurants.

❖ Geauga County Maple Fest (March)
   Enjoy a pancake breakfast, entertainment, and much more on Chardon's main square.
   Website: www.maplefestival.com.

❖ Buzzard Sunday in Hinckley (March)
   Celebrated since 1957, watch for the first sighting of the buzzards as they return to the Buzzard Roost in the Hinckley Reservation of the Cleveland Metroparks.
   Website: www.clemetparks.com.

❖ For more festivals, see the following:
   http://www.positivelycleveland.com

• recreation •

❖ **Beaches**

Cedar Point
One Cedar Point Drive
Sandusky, Ohio
(419) 627-2350

Geneva State Park
4499 Padanarum Road
Geneva, Ohio
(440) 466-8400

Edgewater State Park
6700 Memorial Shoreway
Cleveland, Ohio
(216) 881-8141

Headlands Beach State Park
9601 Headlands Road
Mentor, Ohio
(216) 881-8141

Fairport Harbor Lakefront Park
301 Huntington Rd.
Fairport Harbor, Ohio
(440) 354-4825

Huntington Beach Park
Lake Road (Porter Creek Drive)
Bay Village, Ohio
(216) 351-6300

❖ Get hep! Swing Dancing
Swing dancing at the Bohemian National Hall the last Saturday of every month. Lesson at 8 p.m. Band starts at 9 p.m. $10.00 per person, $8.00 for students with valid ID.
Website: www.gethepswing.com
Ph: (216) 374-1927

Parks and Hiking:

❖ Cleveland Hiking Club (CHC)
The CHC offers over 200 hikes in the Northeast Ohio region on a monthly basis for hikers of all fitness levels. You don't need to be a member of the club to hike.

Website: www.clevelandhikingclub.org

❖ Cuyahoga Valley National Park
Enjoy more than 125 miles of hiking and bike trails. The Ohio and Erie Canal Towpath Trail follows the historic canal and offers great opportunities for biking and walking. At certain points in the park, you can bring your bike aboard the train or just take the train for an enjoyable scenic tour.

Website: www.cvnpa.org. (courtesy of About.com)

· recreation ·

❖ The Emerald Necklace (Part of Cleveland Metroparks)
A 60-mile stretch of parks that starts east of Cleveland, goes south, and then heads back north, ending west of the city, therefore the "Emerald Necklace." Ride your bike, hike, rollerblade, or explore.

Website: www.clemetparks.com
Ph: (216) 635-3200

❖ Nature Center at Shaker Lakes
2600 South Park Boulevard, Cleveland
FREE. Hike a variety of trails in six natural habitats, and enjoy the exhibits at the nature center for free.

Website: http://www.shakerlakes.org/
Ph: (216) 321-5935

❖ Cleveland Metroparks Zoo
Free admission to the zoo on Mondays for Cuyahoga County and Hinckley Township residents (this does not include the Rain Forest exhibit). Proof of residency is required.

Website: www.clemetzoo.com

Skate Parks

❖ Akron Skate Park
1000 Derby Downs Road, Akron, Ohio
Ph: (330) 375-2804

❖ Hudson Skate Park
Corner of Middleton & Stow Road, Hudson, Ohio

❖ North Olmsted Skate Park
5200 Dover Center Road, North Olmsted, Ohio
Ph: (440) 777-8000

❖ North Royalton Skate Park
14600 State Road, North Royalton, Ohio
(South of Route 82, in North Royalton Memorial Park)

❖ For a full list of Ohio Skate Parks and more, go to:
http://www.concretedisciples.com/skateparksdb/display_state.php?state=OH

▪ recreation ▪

Fall Events

HAYRIDES ~ Around Cleveland

- Cleveland Metroparks – Strongsville: Chalet at Valley Parkway, between Routes 42 and 82; (440) 572-9990 – Hayrides given Saturdays and Sundays in October.

- Heavenly Hill Farm – 18375 State Road, North Royalton – (440) 237-8708; Free weekend hayrides (Saturdays and Sundays), kids corn maze, pumpkins, Amish pies/ cider, and pick-your-own apples.

- Luther's Farm Market – 5150 Alger Road, Richfield – (330) 659-2526; The farm offers regular hayrides and haunted hayrides each weekend in October.

- Mapleside Farms – 294 Pearl Rd., Brunswick – (330) 225-5577; Offers horse-drawn hayrides and pony rides, as well as a child-sized hay bale maze, produce for sale, and a gift shop ~ October 1 through October 31.

HAYRIDES ~ Beyond Cleveland

- Heritage Farms – 6050 Riverview Road, Peninsula – (330) 657-2330; Offers hayrides, corn mazes, pumpkins, and mums; Open late September - October 31; Wednesday -Sunday.

- Patterson's Apple Farm – 11414 Caves Road, Chesterland – (440) 729-1964; offers wagon-drawn hayrides to a pumpkin patch; open weekends from mid-September through October.

- Pick n' Save Orchard – 1222 Ledge Road, Medina – (330) 239-1480; enjoy horse-drawn hayrides, tractor-pulled hayrides, a picnic area, and produce for sale (33 miles south of Cleveland).

- Ridgeview Farm Market – 5488 Kinsman Road, State Route 87, Middlefield (32 miles east of Cleveland): (440) 693-4000; Enjoy hayrides, corn maze, pumpkins, and petting zoo. Open Saturday and Sunday from mid-September through October – Middlefield is the 4th-largest Amish settlement in the world.

▪ recreation ▪

Visit Ohio's Amish Country

Ohio's Amish Country is located in the communities of Berlin, Walnut Creek, Sugarcreek, Mount Hope, and Millersburg, Ohio.

Should you decide to visit one of the Amish communities, please keep in mind many businesses are closed on Sundays in observance of the Lord's Day.

Brief History of the Amish:

The Amish are a religious order who emigrated from Switzerland, Alsace (France), and Germany. They traveled to America for religious freedom and first settled in Pennsylvania. The Amish practice a "plain lifestyle" even today, meaning that clothing should be uniform and beards untrimmed, and that the state church should be avoided. Similar in theology to Mennonites, the Amish do not use modern technology, including automobiles and telephones, and they do not believe in medical or life insurance. They also practice excommunication (shunning by all other Amish).

The Amish are best known for their skillfully-kept farms and restaurants featuring superb examples of American home cooking. Still, it is their love for God and Biblical convictions that are at the heart of their lifestyle and practices. Their faith is the foundation of their community. To learn more about the Amish way of life, visit any of the websites below. (Source: Britannica Concise Encyclopedia.com/ Amish.[16])

Helpful Websites ~ All about Amish Country

1. Experience Ohio Amish Country: www.experience-ohio-amish-country.com

2. Ohio's Amish Country and event calendar: www.oacountry.com

3. Driving among the Amish: www.middlefieldohio.com/index.php?option=com_content&task=view&id=14

- tours -

❖ Spring through Fall

NASA Glenn Research Center

FREE tours to the public on the first and third Saturday of the month, April through October. Each tour date shows a different facet of space engineering technology. Reservations required.

NASA Glenn Research Center
21000 Brookpark Road
Cleveland, Ohio 44135 ~ Ph: 216-433-9653

Website: www.nasa.gov/centers/glenn/events/tours.html

❖ Summer

Free Downtown Cleveland Tours:
- Playhouse Square District - Historic Gateway Neighborhood
- Historic Warehouse District - Canal Basin Park

Ph: (216) 771-1994 Website: www.historicagateway.org

❖ Fall

The Ashtabula County Covered Bridge Festival ~ Jefferson, Ohio (October)
The Festival is held the second full weekend in October.

Ph: (440) 576-3769.
Website: www.coveredbridgefestival.org

The Historic Ohio and Erie Canal: The Towpath (Recreational tour ~ all year)
The Towpath is a trail for biking, hiking, horse-backing riding, walking, and jogging. The path begins in Cuyahoga Heights and continues all the way to Peninsula, Ohio, through the Cuyahoga Valley National Park.

Website: www.nps.gov/cuva/ohio-and-erie-canal-towpath-trail.htm

Stan Hywet Hall & Gardens (April – December)
Tour this sixty-five-room Tudor-style mansion and national historic landmark. Located in Akron, it was built in 1912 by Goodyear Rubber Company founder, F. A. Seiberling.

Ph: (330) 836-5533
Website: www.stanhywet.org

▪ tours ▪

❖ The West Side Market

On the edge of Ohio City, the market gives you a glimpse of Cleveland's diverse culture. Enjoy the market's architecture along with fresh produce and meats at reasonable prices. Copy the link below and watch a special Christmas performance at the market.

The Westside Market Christmas 2010: http://www.youtube.com/watch?v=2IGILBxJBJI

Website: www.westsidemarket.org

▪ just for kids ▪

❖ Cuyahoga Valley Church ~ Family Sports Camp (August)

Enjoy one whole week of free activities strictly for kids.

Ph: (440) 746-0404

Website: www.cvconline.org

❖ Children's Museum

Find lots of wonderful exhibits and programs to enhance your child's development. Little ones under 12 months are free!

Ph: (216) 791-7114

Website: www.clevelandchildrensmuseum.org

❖ Polar Bear Days ~ Cleveland Metroparks Zoo

Special discounted admission rates apply for everyone in January when the temperature is below 32° -- "Polar Bear Days." Apply only to admission for the zoo (not the Rain Forest exhibit).

Ph: 216- 661-6500

Website: www.clemetzoo.com ~ logon and see if the day is truly a Polar Bear Day!

❖ Cuyahoga County Public Library System

Find all kinds of free events for your kids at your local public library branch in Cuyahoga County.

Website: http://cuyahogalibrary.org/EventFinder.aspx?TodaysEvents=true

Workspace: Record Other Helpful Ideas That You Discover
~ Events to Enjoy ~

Record Activities, Events, and Outings: Having fun doesn't have to cost a lot of money. Use the space below to record activities you and your family might like to explore. Use the space below to record vacation spots, sporting events, a new sport you'd like to try, or list some of the activities you might like to look into from the last section, Affordable Entertainment.

I honestly think it's the thing I like most, to laugh. It cures a multitude of ills.
— Audrey Hepburn,(1929 – 1993), actress and UNICEF Spokeswoman[17]

Record Leisure Time Activities and Goals for a Healthier Life: Recreation and leisure time is an important part of a well-balanced life. We certainly can't work all week without taking time to refresh our bodies and our minds. Use the space below to record any new habits or goals you would like to establish to make your life better. Some ideas might be working in the garden, working out at the gym, or walking in the park three times a week.

Record Cultural Activities: If you'd like, record any movies, plays, or other activities that spark your interest. Try something new. You just may love it ~ and love your life even more!

I love Mickey Mouse more than any woman I've ever known.
– *Walt Disney (1901-1966), motion picture producer
and pioneer of animated cartoon films*[18]

Two type of voices command
your attention today.

Negative ones fill your mind with
doubt, bitterness, and fear.

Positive ones purvey hope and strength.
Which one will you choose to heed?

*– Max Lucado, "America's Pastor" per Christianity Today
magazine, author, and writer (b. 1955)*[19]

Soothing the Soul: Tips for Emotional Well-being

… every thought, word,
and behavior affects
our greater health and well-being.

– Greg Anderson, author and founder of the American wellness project (b. 1964)[20]

Happy, Healthy, and Whole

This section contains a collection of suggestions for your mind, body, and spirit.

In the first part, "It's All in Your State of *Mind,*" you will find ways to achieve mental clarity. Read through the second part, "Every *Body* Needs," for ways to feel your best physically. And finally, in the last section part, "Let Your *Spirit* Rise," discover new ways to feel great emotionally.

Please use these entries as a guide through your experience (Isaiah 43:1-3*a*). And above all else, continue to read and meditate on God's Word. It is the bright star that will guide you.

God has already given you everything you need to be successful, now and for every other season of your life. On your journey, you will learn many things and meet people along the way who will need your help. You will need theirs as well. Please, however, do not let pride be your companion as you walk along the trail. Pride will only hold you back from receiving the countless blessings that God so wants to give to you.

Use these suggestions to help maximize your coping skills and sustain your overall well-being as you move forward. You already have the victory! God bless you!

~~~~~~

Note: In this text, the word "spirit," in the last section, "Let Your <u>Spirit</u> Rise," refers to your emotional well-being. It refers to how you are functioning and ultimately how you are coping with life's challenges. The goal of each little item in this section is to help you feel your best, mentally, physically, and emotionally.

It's All in Your State of *Mind*

On this page: Your words have great power. They affect your thinking, feelings, and ultimately, your behavior.

~~~~~~

1. Speak words that are positive; they have great power!

    You can't speak words of defeat and failure yet expect to live in victory.[21] Because whether you realize it or not, your words have great power. Take that a step further, and you will also find that the words you speak to yourself (self-talk) have great power in directing your happiness and success in life. Therefore, what you say to yourself should always be positive and hopeful. Why? Because you'll believe the things you tell yourself more than anything else.

    Words are containers. They can hold emotions, ideas, and thoughts. They have the ability to either bless or harm someone. Words are powerful. Christian author and speaker, Joyce Meyer, puts it this way: "Words are containers for power and they carry either creative or destructive power."[22] Creflo Dollar, TV evangelist and founder and senior pastor of World Changers Church International (WCCI) in College Park, Georgia, puts it very plainly: "When you understand the role your words play in your life's outcome, you will become mindful of what you say every day."[23]

    Joel Osteen, in his book *Your Best Life Now,* explains,

    > Words are similar to seeds. By speaking them aloud, they are planted in our subconscious minds and they take on a life of their own; they take root, grow, and produce fruit of the same kind. If we speak positive words, our lives will move in that direction. Similarly, negative words will produce poor results. We can't speak words of defeat and failure yet expect to live in victory. We will reap exactly what we sow.

    > When times are tough, human nature tends to want to complain, to talk about the problem, to tell everyone who will listen how badly life is treating us. But such conversations are self-defeating. To get through a tough time quicker and with better results, we must learn to speak as positively as possible.[24]

It's All in Your State of *Mind*

On this page: What are you focused on today? Your life will go in the direction of your thoughts. Your best bet is to develop a sense of gratitude and keep hope alive.

~~~~~~

2. What you focus on expands.

   What you think about (focus on) matters. Why? It's simple. Your thoughts become your words and your words become your behavior. Pay attention to what you're thinking about.

3. Remove all mental clutter from your life and keep running your race with determination –motivational coach Kevin Elko, Ph.D., author of *The Pep Talk*.[25]

   To remove mental clutter you can make a list of things you are dealing with and prioritize projects. Most importantly, keep your focus on the events in front of you today (Hebrews 12:1,11; Luke 6:38; Psalms 34:9 - 10).

4. Change your perspective. Develop a sense of GRATITUDE.

   Verbalize five things you are grateful for each night before you go to bed. This will help change your focus and you'll so soon feel better emotionally. The verse from Philippians 4:8 says it so well. Whatever is true, whatever is honorable, whatever is right, whatever is pure, whatever is lovely, whatever is of good repute – let your mind dwell on these things.

5. *Hope* is belief in a positive outcome to your circumstances.

   Hope means you're expecting something good – you're looking for something to show up in the future. It's a confident feeling that the tide will soon turn – and it will! To keep hope alive, read something uplifting about God right before bed.

   "When you do nothing, you feel overwhelmed and powerless. But when you get involved, you feel the sense of hope and accomplishment that comes from knowing you are working to make things better."
       – Pauline R. Kezer (former Connecticut State Legislator and teacher)[26]

It's All in Your State of *Mind*

On this page: Believe the glass is half full, record your thoughts and ideas in a journal, and set goals. Mix these well and enjoy a healthy and satisfying life.

~~~~~~

6. Positive words, thoughts, and being around other positive people will keep you feeling hopeful.

   Being positive elevates your mood and makes difficult tasks seem more possible and within your reach. For lots of encouraging thoughts, read Joel Osteen's book, *Your Best Life Now: 7 Steps to Living Your Full Potential.*

7. Gain a better understanding of yourself by keeping a journal.

   Journaling has nothing to do with your writing skills; rather, it is a means to help you balance perspective, release stress and negative emotions, explore new options, and appreciate your accomplishments. Why is this so important? In the hustle and bustle of daily living it is increasingly difficult, sometimes impossible, to find quiet moments when you can reflect. A journal encourages you to take time for reflection.

   Keeping a journal is especially helpful when you have a change in lifestyle – job loss, birth in the family, or death of a loved one. All you need is a hardcover book with paper and the same time each day to write (Thanks to Lois Guarino's *Writing Your Authentic Self.* [27])

8. Set goals for your life.

   Goals give you something to work toward. You will achieve more if you write out your ideas and goals. Make sure you review them daily (Habakkuk 2:2-3). Joel Osteen, in his sermon aired on TV February 2008, "Making Plans to Succeed," suggested that you have a vision for your life. Osteen emphasizes that you don't have to see right now how it will all work out. We set our plans, but God directs our steps (Proverbs 16:9).

It's All in Your State of Mind

On this page: Embrace the concepts below. They will help you respond to life events in positive ways and give you the success you need.

~~~~~~

9. Do you see things as problems or challenges?

   A problem can seem like something you will never be able to solve – no answers, just something that keeps you mentally stuck so that you cannot move forward.

   But try labeling something as a challenge. Then it has quite a different effect on your ability to get going. When you call something a challenge, mentally that conveys that you can work through it step-by-step and motivate yourself until the situation is completely resolved. It can cause you to stretch your abilities, work harder, and dig in a little more.

10. "However you call a thing controls your response to it," ~ Bishop Eddie Long.

    In other words, if you say something is a crisis, you'll behave in that way. And if you say something is an adventure, your actions and thoughts will respond to it in exactly that way as well. From Bishop Long ~ on his Trinity Broadcast Network show late February, 2009.

11. Choose to have a good attitude, especially during difficult times.

    How's your attitude? Biblical principles teach us that a good attitude determines how long you will stay in your present situation. The Israelites wandered in the desert for forty years before they inherited the Promised Land. Why did it take them so long? Lack of confidence, fear, and not trusting God are a few of the reasons. And probably one could even guess that during those forty years they became negative and complained, which made things even worse.

    Today, realize your present situation is here to help you. Therefore, start praising God and put away self-pity. Read Numbers 13-14.

It's All in Your State of *Mind*

~~~~~~

12. Don't rely on your feelings!

Your feelings can be so deceiving. One moment you can feel on top of the world, the next moment you can feel discouraged or depressed. Feelings can cause you to shrink back in fear instead of seizing your moment of triumph. When you remember fear is actually false evidence appearing real, that should encourage you and help you respond differently. Christian teacher and speaker, Joyce Meyer, *on her TV show*, Enjoying Everyday Life, shared, "Control your feelings; don't live by them. Live by the Word of God!"[28]

No matter what your present situation, choose to respond to it in a positive way. Don't rely on your feelings. Instead, have faith. God will do the rest!

13. Live life to the fullest each day.

In Africa, to go on a *safari* – the Swahili word for journey – is to leave the comfort and safety of civilization to venture into the wilderness. "You could expect many things of God at night when the campfire burned before the tents," Beryl Markham wrote about safari life. "The world is there and you are here…Each day in the wilderness brings with it the struggle to survive and a heightened awareness of how wonderful it is to see the sun set and rise again in the morning." Each day on safari is lived to the fullest because it is all that is guaranteed. If only we could learn this lesson as well in our everyday lives.[29]

14. Is this action moving me toward a more powerful place?

Keep this thought where you can see it during the day. This will help you keep priorities straight and will remind you to focus on what's important today and what can wait for tomorrow. (Susan Jeffers, *Feel the Fear and Do It Anyway*).[30]

It's All in Your State of *Mind*

On this page: Faith is a powerful tool. However, fear is equally as powerful. The one you choose to acknowledge will determine where you end up.

~~~~~~

15. Faith or fear – how do you respond?

Faith is the opposite of fear. Faith says, "I believe, even though I don't yet see it in my life." And like fear, faith, too, is a choice. With life constantly changing, there's always a new fork in the road – that place where we must decide how to proceed and how we will behave.

Faith requires courage. But courage doesn't mean you're not afraid. It just means you are CHOOSING to believe the best of God and the situation. Faith elevates you to a place where you can still enjoy your life even when things are not perfect and have not yet been completely resolved or answered. Faith tests everything you are, everywhere you've been, and everything you know at this present moment. Faith says, "I trust you, God!"

Fear, on the other hand, will rob you of your joy in life. It can cause you to make poor decisions and lose your creativity. It will paralyze you so that you don't take action, or you will shrink back from new opportunities because you don't believe you can handle them.

Take this advice: Don't give in to fear! Read II Timothy 1:7.

A preacher on Moody radio urged listeners to cultivate a courageous heart by placing their situations entirely in God's hands; then, trust that God will do what's best. Further, EXPECT God to step into your situation (Psalms 55:12). It also doesn't really matter if you can see God in your situation – what matters is that God sees you. Read Isaiah 43:1-3.

Every *Body* Needs

On this page: See what's important for good physical health.

~~~~~~

1. Get seven to eight hours of sleep each night. This helps your brain function to its maximum capacity, and you'll feel so much better too!

2. Exercise at least three times a week. Walking is one of the best exercises for you. Walking helps reduce stress, and since it is a weight-bearing exercise, you'll be strengthening your bones as well! However, whatever exercise you like is the one you should do. Why? Because you'll stick with it!

3. Eat fresh fruits and vegetables, whole grains, lean meats and fish, plus plant-based protein like lentils, peanut butter, dried beans, nuts, and tofu. Avoid processed foods that contain sodium and additives. After age 50, the body has a difficult time digesting wheat and dairy products. You may want to avoid them.

4. Take a multi-vitamin. Doctors now suggest taking a daily multi-vitamin, because we don't always get the vitamins and minerals needed in our diet.

5. Drink water throughout the day. Your cells, especially your brain cells, need water. Dehydration can cause headaches and poor brain functioning.

6. To improve your memory and maintain healthy brain functioning, keep learning new information so that the brain makes new connections. This is called "lifelong learning" – learn a new instrument, a new language, take dance lessons, or take up a new hobby. A good night's sleep, regular exercise, thinking positively, gratitude, and social connections all help to improve your brain functioning. Drink water and take fish oil (Omega-3 fatty acids).

Try these simple things in your daily life to challenge your brain: sit in a different chair at the dinner table, brush your teeth with the opposite hand, sleep on the other side of the bed, and light a candle before an activity, you'll remember it better. Develop the habit of actively paying attention and repeating to yourself what you want to remember. (See University Hospital's, "Maximize Your Memory" and Dr. Daniel Amen's book, *Change Your Brain, Change Your Life.*)[31]

Every *Body* Needs

On this page: Here's the very latest on sugar, caffeine, and getting back to the basics when life gets crazy. Find information, too, on the winter blues.

~~~~~~

7. Say no to sugar. It has no nutritional value for your body.

    In the short term, sugar will provide the body with more energy. But later it will cause a dip in energy. Therefore, avoid sugar especially during times of stress.

8. Avoid caffeine.

    Caffeine raises the level of stress hormones, making you irritable. And for some, it can affect the ability to sleep.

9. Has life gotten a little crazy lately?

    When things are out of sorts, get back to the basics of good health. This includes reading God's Word, getting your rest and exercise, eating well, and avoiding sugar (and anything else that promotes good health and well-being for you).

10. Got the winter blues?

    In the winter many of us are affected by Seasonal Affective Disorder, or SAD. The lack of sunlight hinders the brain's ability to make a chemical called serotonin. Low levels of serotonin can cause you to feel sluggish and depressed. To improve your well-being take a walk in the early morning hours when there is sun and increase your intake of Omega-3 fatty acids by eating oily fish like salmon, herring, and sardines. Also make sure your diet includes at least 800 units of Vitamin D daily and foods rich in Vitamin C.

    If you are still experiencing problems after monitoring your diet and exercise, see your doctor. Therapeutic light boxes may be recommended (no UV rays).[32]

Let Your *Spirit* Rise

On this page: Try these seven strategies to improve your emotional well-being.

~~~~~~

1. Avoid watching the news every night. Its negativity will cause you to be fearful.

2. Don't pay bills, look at finances, or review your mail right before you go to bed.

3. Take time to tidy up.

    Research shows that unmade beds, dirty dishes, and piles of laundry are stressful reminders of unfinished business. A quick clean-up session will boost your mood and give you a sense of accomplishment.

4. What are the miracles God has already done in your life?

    Looking at what you have and where you've been is helpful. Make a list of the great things God has already done for you. This will give you hope for what you need today and for the future. Especially look at the many creative ways God has answered your prayers and blessed you.

5. Start an encouragement file ~ Read it once a week or more if needed.

    Sometimes there are people who encourage us, but for the most part, we must continue to encourage ourselves. Therefore, save cards and notes that others have given you. Write down the great comments also that people have made about you. Reviewing these will encourage you and keep you focused on the right things. More importantly, read God's Word and hold on to His promises.

6. Recount the many miracles in the Bible.

    Focusing on all the miracles in the Bible will encourage your spirit. They should remind you that nothing is impossible for God. Read Ephesians 3:20.

7. Light candles and enjoy the light and beauty they provide. Light one, then pray.

Let Your *Spirit* Rise

On this page: More ways to feel good and stay in the flow of life.

~~~~~~

8. Go out to dinner, lunch, or coffee about once a week.

    Going out will give you something to look forward to, and the change of scenery (instead of eating in front of the TV if your single) will lift your spirits. If going out for dinner seems too overwhelming financially, try just going out for coffee. Whatever you decide to do, get out and enjoy the people and new surroundings! You'll feel better.

9. Maintain the traditional or customary things in your life, especially during difficult times.

    It is important to stay in the flow of life. This means celebrate birthdays, Christmas, etc., as usual. Yes, you should still get out there and buy or make a few things for your family members and friends during the holidays. Shop the sales and employ a little creativity. Above all else, don't give in to fear. Enjoy your life instead of letting fear rob you of the present moment. Trust God.

10. Invite others over for a potluck dinner or dessert some evening.

    Potlucks are a great way to get together with others and will fend off isolation during the winter. Having others bring a dish will help with the cost, and being around others will boost your morale. Social connections are important for healthy brain functioning too

11. Take a walk in the morning hours to help boost your mood

    In the winter months in areas where there are few sunny days, exposure to the sun for fifteen minutes (without sunscreen) during a walk helps the body produce Vitamin D and serotonin. Serotonin is an important chemical made in the brain that helps fend off depression. (See #10 in "Every *Body* Needs.")

Let Your *Spirit* Rise

On this page: Take a sixty-second mental vacation and get rid of your stress. And back by popular demand, get out your paper and pen to send a thank-you note or one of encouragement. It's so true — you always reap what you sow!

~~~~~~

12. Enjoy a sixty-second vacation. It will help your stress melt away.

    Take a sixty-second vacation. This will rejuvenate you mentally, and its relaxing effects will help relieve and reduce stress. You can do this anywhere; except DON'T DO THIS WHILE DRIVING (or at a stop sign)!

    a. First, take a few deep breaths. Breathe out s-l-o-w-l-y.
    b. Close your eyes and simply relax in a chair.
    c. See yourself in your favorite vacation spot or a place you've always wanted to visit.
    d. Notice everything around you and enjoy!
    e. RELAX for about thirty to sixty seconds, enjoying your lovely vacation spot. Observe colors, textures, environment, people, and more.
    f. Gradually return to the present moment.

13. Write a letter or send a sweet note to someone you know. This will lift their spirit – and yours as well!

    Everyone needs encouragement and needs to know that someone cares about them. E-mail has changed our culture. However, you can revive this caring practice by putting notes in Christmas stockings, lunch boxes, or sending a card. If you are really ambitious, you can make your own cards. Being creative may inspire you to take up a new hobby or serve as a good way to interact with teens and other family members.

Let Your *Spirit* Rise

On this page: Doing one thing differently today could put a little zing in your life! When you get your mind off yourself and volunteer to help somebody else, you'll be amazed at how good you feel about you!

~~~~~~

14. Do one thing differently.

Do one thing differently in your day. Could it really make you feel better – or even great? An example of this might be to drive a different way to church. By driving a different way, you will notice different shops, restaurants, people, houses, and trees and flowers along the way. Doing one thing differently will actually give you an emotional lift by providing the brain with different stimuli to process. What you will find is this: you'll get to your destination feeling emotionally encouraged. Depending on your level of appreciation, at the end of the day, you will still be feeling the positive effects of doing just one thing differently! Try it (suggestion from psychologist Dr. Robin Smith, as seen on The Oprah Winfrey Show, 2009)!

15. Volunteer.

Giving of your time and talents will take your mind off yourself. The good feelings that giving create will increase your self-esteem. A volunteer position is also a great thing to include on your resume. If you are job hunting, it will show any perspective employer that you are motivated and that you use your time wisely. And the contacts you make could be used as references. In some cases, volunteering can lead to full-time employment.

Besides church-sponsored volunteer activities, another resource is Business Volunteers Unlimited, an organization that provides a wide range of opportunities to help others in this area. In 2007, HandsOn Northeast Ohio was formed to address the increased need in our community. You can contact them at www. handsonneo.org if you are interested in volunteering. Marymount Hospital is also often in need of volunteers. Contact them at (216) 587-8131.

Let Your *Spirit* Rise

Question: What do extra time, candlelight, and being positive all have in common?

Answer: You can achieve some special moments with all of them. They can elevate the good feelings present in your life.

~~~~~~

16. Plug in projects you've been wanting to do in your extra time.

    While you are waiting for things to materialize in your life, work on projects you have been meaning to work on, like scrapbooks, photo albums, address books, recipe files, or updating your iPod. You'll feel a sense of satisfaction from finally getting these things done! These activities can increase self-esteem and provide a great feeling of accomplishment.

17. Candlelight makes any time special.

    Light candles, and then begin your time of prayer. Why candlelight? If you do anything out of the ordinary that makes the event more memorable. Joyce Meyer, Christian author and speaker, time and again conveys to her audiences that trusting in God always means there will be unanswered questions. But keep praying and seeking God. Amen!

18. Being a **POSITIVE** person is a great asset!

    Positive people draw other people to them! Why? Because we like people who are upbeat and hopeful! They're great to be around. So, to help you stay upbeat, surround yourself with other believers who will encourage you and strengthen your faith. Socializing will keep you from feeling isolated, especially during the winter months. And whether you are looking for a job or are currently employed, upcoming parties and get-togethers will give you something to look forward to. They can also be a great place to do some networking! And this will help keep you positive and hopeful about your situation until things change.

Let Your *Spirit* Rise

<u>*On this page:*</u>   It's important to have something to look forward to – a party, a cookout, or miniature golf. The benefits of interacting with others cannot be underestimated. Or, go and visit Aunt Molly. It's always good to make someone else smile.

~~~~~~

19. Being with others is a good thing!

Plan a potluck dinner and swap goods, services, and coupons with friends and family. When you clean out your cupboards and drawers, I'll bet you'll find many great things that someone else could use. Swap them or give them to others at a potluck. This event can meet both your need to socialize (be with others and fend off isolation) as well as help to provide you with useful items. This is a resourceful way to help save money. Just bring dinner, and you don't have to spend a dime! Enjoy!

20. Surround yourself with great people!

If you're the smartest one in your group, your group is too small. Find another group. Find people who are smarter than you. That's because they will challenge you and help you stretch to the next level. Proverbs 27:17 in the Bible says, "Iron sharpens iron. He who walks with the wise becomes wise." Therefore, choose your friends carefully so that you can rise higher. (Thanks to Joel Osteen.)[33]

21. Discouraged? Who gives you encouragement?

From time to time we all get discouraged. That's why you should surround yourself with people who are positive and lift you up emotionally. Sometimes, however, we have to encourage ourselves. And that's just the time to dig into your encouragement file and do just that. For more information, see item #6, in the beginning of this section.

But when you feel down, start praising God. Take your eyes off your problems too, and read His Word. You'll feel so much better. Taking a walk or putting on some great music, will also help lift your mood.

Let Your *Spirit* Rise

On this page: Laughter puts life into perspective. Check out the quotes below.
They are full of wisdom and power!

~~~~~~

22. Laughter is good medicine for the soul!

Did you know that laughter can reduce your stress? And even if you fake a laugh, your immune system will benefit. Having a sense of humor is very important too!

23. Great quotes to inspire you.

God's Word is more powerful than anything anyone can tell you. But here are some thoughts and quotes that you may find helpful or amusing.

❖ Courage doesn't always roar. Sometimes courage is the quiet voice at the end of the day saying, "I will try again tomorrow." – *Mary Anne Radmacher* [34]

❖ Our problem is really not our problems: It's how we respond to them. – *Joyce Meyer* [35]

❖ If I have the belief that I can do it, I shall surely acquire the capacity to do it, even if I do not have it at the beginning. – *Mohandas Gandhi* [36]

❖ You can be either pitiful or powerful. But not both! – *Joyce Meyer* [37]

❖ She may be just a fish, but Dory in the movie *Finding Nemo* certainly has the right idea: Keep swimming! [38]

24. Kindness is a great thing! It brings a little love to those along the way!

Be kind to yourself! Then, you'll find that you give the gift of kindness to others too! Kind words are like honey…good for your health. (See Proverbs 16:24.)

25. God's Presence

God loves you and He has a great plan for your life. Make it a practice to look carefully throughout your day for evidence of God's love, care, and power.

Workspace: Record Other Soothing Ideas You Discover
~ Emotions and Behavior ~

Record Thoughts and Emotions to Become a Healthier You: The more you know about yourself and why you do things, the healthier you will be. Use the space below to record any emotions that are causing you distress or keeping you from reaching your goals and moving forward (for example: fear, stress, unforgiveness, or a negative attitude).

Record More About Your Thoughts, Your Life, or Your Feelings: Your goal is to be a healthy individual. Negative emotions can rob you of joy, love, and the ability to give to others. They can also rob you of blessings that God so wants to give you. Use the space below to record your thoughts about how your life is unfolding right now.

The remarkable thing is we have a choice everyday regarding the attitude we will embrace for that day. – *Charles R. Swindol, American writer/clergyman (b.1934)*[39]

Record Positive Self-talk: Self-talk is what you say to yourself. Self-talk should be positive words you repeatedly say to yourself. For example, I did a great job today. I'm proud of myself for completing the job. I CAN do it! Now it's your turn to record below some great words to feed you mind, heart, and your soul.

Record Distractions: Putting your thoughts or concerns down on paper clears your mind. With God's help it can be a way to find the answers you need. That's because the process of recording your concerns yields greater mental clarity. Record below anything that will free up your mind including concerns, feelings, challenges, or decisions you need to make.

"You're braver than you believe, stronger than you seem, and smarter than you think."
– *Christopher Robin to Pooh, from the children's book series,*
Winnie-the-Pooh*, by A. A. Milne (1882-1956)*[40]

More
Fresh Hope
Resources

Four things let us ever keep in mind:

God hears prayer,
God heeds prayer,
God answers prayer,
and God delivers by prayer.

– *E. M. Bounds,* (1835 (1835-08-15) – 1913), *clergyman and author* [41]

Prayer

Prayer is simply talking to God and telling Him how you feel and what you need. Your words do not have to be fancy or in any particular fashion. You just have to be honest and sincere as you pray. Prayers that are based on the Word of God are the most powerful. And of course, offering praise to God is a great way to start your time of prayer.

Prayer is the most powerful resource you possess. It's powerful because It allows God to move in your life; it unleashes His power. Prayer can give comfort and peace of mind when you tell God your concerns. In fact, Scripture tells us in I Peter 5:7, "Cast all your cares on God because He cares for you." And while the answers may not come overnight, keep praying. When all is silent, your Heavenly Father is most at work in your life. Do you need a miracle today? God is there now waiting to help you. Whatever your circumstances are, keep looking for the rainbow from your window – it will soon be there. Because God does answer prayers!

Please submit your prayer requests to the ministries below and on the next page. You may go online, or call the phone numbers below to connect with a caring Christian for prayer.

1. Benny Hinn Ministries

    Submit prayer requests on the home page via the "Prayer" tab at the top.

    Website: www.bennyhinn.org.

2. Christian Broadcasting Network (CBN)

    Submit your prayer requests and you'll receive a caring reply from founder, Pat Robertson.

    Toll-free number: 1-800-759-0700

    Website: www.cbn.com.

Prayer

3. Creflo Dollar Ministries

   Toll-free number: 1-866-477-7683 (for immediate attention)

   Submit your prayer requests on the home page, look under "Contact" for prayer requests.

   Website: www.creflodollarministries.org

4. Jentezen Franklin Media Ministries

   Submit requests under "Prayer Center," located in the "My Community" tab.

   Website: http://www.jentezenfranklin.org/contact/prayer-request.php

5. Joyce Meyer Ministries

   On the bottom of the home page, find "Contact Us." Then select "Request Prayer" for submission of prayer requests.

   Toll-free number: 1-866-349-3300

   Website: www.joycemeyer.org

6. Marilyn Hickey Ministries

   Submit your requests for prayer through their website.

   Website: www.marilynandsarah.org

7. Rod Parsley Ministries

   To submit prayer requests on their home page, go to "Ministry Center," then "Prayer & Praise."

   Website: www.rodparsley.com

Prayer and Counseling

1. CHRISTIAN BROADCASTING NETWORK (CBN)

   CBN's website has a complete counseling referral section. Click on "Prayer Request" near the CBN logo at the top of the page. This will take you into the "Prayer and Counseling" section.

   Great articles also on this site: (To find them, use "SEARCH" - upper left):

   - Reaching Out to Survivors of Suicide
   - Family-Related Articles to Equip You with Information
   - "Help for Discouragement" – article by Pastor Rick Warren

   Website: www.cbn.com

2. HOPE FOR THE HEART – Providing Truth for Today's Problems

   Website: www.hopefortheheart.org

   Phone: 1-800-488-HOPE (4673), Monday-Friday: 7:30 a.m. - 1:30 a.m., CST

3. ON-RADIO COUNSELING HELP

   - Hope in the Night, two-hour live show with call-ins Monday-Friday.
   Phone: 1-800-644-4817 (or visit the website)

   - *Hope for the Heart*, thirty-minute show that discusses a different topic each week. See the website for more.

   Website: www.hopefortheheart.org

4. PRAYER and more about a RELATIONSHIP WITH GOD (Moody Radio)

   Website: www.needhim.org

   Call Toll-free 1-888-NEED HIM (1-888-633-3446)

Workspace: Record Your Prayer Requests Here
~ Pray ▪ It Unleashes God's Power! ~

Record Your Own Prayer Requests: Record your own prayer requests below.

Record Any Other Requests or Concerns: Record below the prayer requests that burden your heart today. Those requests may include praying for acquaintances, friends, family, healing, churches, ministries, governments, organizations, work place situations, communities, states, nations, our world, unsaved individuals, and those being persecuted.

Prayer is the place where burdens change shoulders.
– marquee of the North Royalton Baptist Church

Workspace: Record the Answers to Your Prayers
~ God Answers Prayer! ~

How Does God Answer Our Prayers?

(Words of wisdom from Emma, my little field mouse ~ Emma's story and picture are in the social service agency section in Part I.) Here's what she wants you to know:

Loving us so much, God blesses us and answers our prayers when the time is right – and after we have asked Him so kindly, sometimes night after night. God's timing is always perfect. So if you haven't had an answer yet to your prayers, remember, truly glorious things take time and preparation. That's so they unfold in just the right way.

But don't worry. God has not forgotten you. He's busy now attending to every one of your needs. And when everything has been brought together, you'll receive the answers in a most unexpected and miraculous way!

Record below some of the wonderful ways God has answered your prayers.

God answers our prayers in the most delicious way! [42]
– Emma, my little field mouse, blessed by God with her favorite chocolate brownies.

Out of difficulties grow miracles.

– Jean De La Bruyere, French satiric moralist (1645 - 1696)[43]

Emergency Hotline Numbers & Websites

►Dial 9-1-1 for Immediate Medical Emergency Attention◄

If you or a loved one is having difficulties, help is just a phone call or click of the mouse away. Reaching out for help shows great strength. You'll be glad you did!

1. AL-ANON: HELP AND HOPE FOR FAMILIES OF ALCOHOLICS

    Cleveland Area Al-Anon Information Services
    Phone: (216) 621-1381
    Website: www.afgcleveland.org

2. ALCOHOLICS ANONYMOUS

    If you are having trouble controlling your drinking and realize that you need help, Alcoholics Anonymous (AA) can help you. A short quiz on their website will help you to determine if you are suffering from alcoholism. According to their website, "there is no disgrace in having a problem."
    Website: www.aa.org

3. DOMESTIC VIOLENCE AND ABUSE

    Advocates are available for victims and for anyone calling on their behalf.

    National Domestic Violence Hotline
    24-hour access for all 50 states. Translators available.

    Phone: 1–800–799–SAFE (7233) or TTY 1–800–787–3224.
    Cleveland Hotline Phone: *(216)* 391-4357
    Battered Women Hotline Phone: (216) 391-4357
    Website: www.ndvh.org

4. DRUG & ALCOHOL INFORMATION SERVICES

    Referral through United Way's *First Call for Help:*
    Phone: (216) 436-2000 or 2-1-1

Emergency Hotline Numbers & Websites

5. EATING DISORDER TREATMENT

   The term "eating disorder" applies to a range of disorders that are most easily and outwardly recognized as affecting the eating habits of an individual. Eating disorders may affect people in any age group, regardless of gender.

   Website: www.eatingdisorderscleveland.org

6. ELDER ABUSE HOTLINE

   Local Hotline Phone: (216) 420-6700

   National Hotline Phone: 1-(800) 252-8966

7. GAMBLERS ANONYMOUS

   Gamblers Anonymous is a self-help, 12-Step Program that offers support meetings on a worldwide basis. You can request an information packet via e-mail. Include name and mailing address in your request.

   Website: www.gamblersanonymous.org

8. INHALANT ABUSE

   One in five children will abuse inhalants by the eighth grade. Learn how to prevent and treat victims of abuse.

   Inhalant Abuse Prevention Kit: Designed to educate parents of elementary and middle-schoolers to talk to their children about the dangers and risks associated with inhalants. Website: http://inhalant.org/resources/

9. MENTAL ILLNESS

   National Alliance on Mental Illness:

   Website:www.nami.org

10. MISSING & EXPLOITED CHILDREN

    National Hotline: 1-800-843-5678

Emergency Hotline Numbers & Websites

11. NURSE ON CALL: CLEVELAND CLINIC FOUNDATION

    Skilled nurses will access your medical condition and direct you towards proper treatment if necessary. Hotline: (216) 444-1234

12. PORNOGRAPHY ADDICTION WORKSHOP: X3 PURE

    A 30-day workshop for men, women, and teens designed to bring recovery from pornography addiction. From their website: "It is time you ended your fantasy world and enjoyed true intimacy in your life. Private, online, and effective, x3pure can help you end the downward spiral of shame, alienation, and sin."

    Website: http://x3watch.com/x3pure.html

13. (Pornography) PARENTAL CONTROL SOFTWARE: SAFE EYES

    Software blocks pornography, filters the content of YouTube and online TV, and monitors social networking (Facebook, chat, etc.). Works on up to three computers in one household. Dave Ramsey, financial expert, has endorsed this software.

    Website: http://x3watch.com/safeeyes.html

14. PORNOGRAPHY ACCOUNTABILITY SOFTWARE: X3 WATCH

    X3Watch software records the name, time, and date that websites containing questionable material are accessed. An accountability partner is chosen and notified of all questionable sites the user visits each month.

    Website: http://x3watch.com/x3watch.html

15. PORNOGRAPHY ADDICTIONS (SUPPORT FOR OVERCOMING)

    Online resource designed to provide accountability, encouragement, and help.
    Website: http://xxxchurch.com/

Emergency Hotline Numbers & Websites

16. POISON CONTROL – Toll-Free Number: 1-800-222-1222

In January 2002, the government pubished this toll-free poison control number that serves all states, cities, and townships. This number automatically connects callers to their local poison control center for FREE, twenty-four hours a day, seven days a week.

When calling, you'll need:
- Victim's age and weight – this can affect how quickly poisons operate
- Precise item ingested – refer to the bottle's label for the exact name and ingredients
- Approximate amount of poison ingested
- How long ago the poison was ingested
- Condition of the victim – groggy, hyperactive, nauseous, etc.
- How victim was exposed to the poison: ingestion, vapors, skin contact, etc.
- Medical concerns such as allergies or medication that could interfere with the poison or its treatment

17. PREGNANCY COUNSELING – Abortion Clinic Alternatives

Five local centers offer peer counseling and accurate information about all pregnancy options; however, they do not offer or refer for abortion services.

Website: www.northcoastphc.org

18. RAPE CRISIS INTERVENTION

Cleveland Rape Crisis Center

Phone: (216) 579-0703 or (216) 619-6194; Monday-Friday: 9 a.m. - 5 p.m.)

After-Hours Hotline: (216) 619-6192

19. SELF INJURY HELPLINE

Hotline: 1-800-DONT-CUT

Emergency Hotline Numbers & Websites

20. SOCIAL SERVICES – CHILD ABUSE HOTLINE

    Hotline: 1-800-342-3720

21. SUICIDE PREVENTION ACTION NETWORK

    Website: www.spanusa.org

22. SUICIDE PREVENTION HOTLINE – CLEVELAND, OHIO

    • 24-Hour Crisis Hotline – (216) 623-6888

    • The Together Hotline – The Free Clinic of Greater Cleveland
      Crisis Intervention & Referral Service
      Open every night from 8:00 p.m. to midnight: (216) 721-1115

23. USA NATIONAL SUICIDE HOTLINES

    Toll-free / 24 hours / 7 days a week

    Hotline: 1-800-SUICIDE

24. SURVIVING SUICIDE (Healing: After the Loss of a Loved One to Suicide)

    Website: www.survivingsuicide.com

25. VIDEO GAME ADDICTION

    Website: www.video-game-addiction.org

Record Medical Advice Here: On any given day, anyone could need help. Medical emergencies can spring out of nowhere. Use this page to record any medical information or directions you may have received from a nurse, doctor, counselor, or other trained medical professional. If you are having a medical emergency, call 9-1-1 immediately.

Record Medical Concerns and Questions Here: Record below any questions you have or information you'd like to share with your doctor or other medical professional.

If you judge people, you have no time to love them. – *Mother Theresa*[44]

He who has health, has hope. And he who has hope, has everything.
– *Publilius Syrus (Roman author, 1st century BC)* [45]

Workspace: Record Helpful Information Here
~ Decide to Be a Blessing ~

Record Ways You Can Bless Others: Did you know that giving out three sincere compliments during the day can make you and the other person feel like a million bucks? Compliments are small bundles of love that bless others. Make sure you give out some every day. It's also great to give out a big smile with your compliments as well! Use the space below to record some great compliments you'd like to give to somebody this week.

One kind word can warm three winter months. – *Japanese proverb*[46]

Health is a state of complete
physical, mental, and social well-being,
and not merely the absence
of disease or infirmity.

– Author unknown[47]

For Those Touched by
· *Cancer and/or Disability* ·

CANCER:

The Gathering Place, at its two locations, provides a variety of therapeutic programs and information for adults, children, and family members dealing with cancer. All services are free of charge.

- ❖ The Gathering Place East
  The Arnold & Sydell Miller Family Campus
  23300 Commerce Park
  Beachwood, Ohio 44122

  The Gathering Place West
  800 Sharon Drive
  Westlake, Ohio 44145

  Ph: (216) 595-9546 - for both locations
  Website: www.touchedbycancer.org

Located in Akron, Stewart's Caring Place also provides support for those dealing with cancer.

- ❖ Stewart's Caring Place (near Summit Mall)
  2955 West Market Street, Suite R
  Akron, Ohio 44333

  Ph: (330) 836-1772
  Website: info@stewartscaringplace.com

For Those Touched by
▪ *Cancer and/or Disability* ▪

DISABILITY:

The Ohio Rehabilitation Services Commission (RSC) is a state agency that helps those with a physical and/or mental disability gain employment, independence, and Social Security disability determination outcomes. Visit their website at: www.rsc.ohio.gov. The RSC provides help based on eligibility through the Bureau of Vocational Rehabilitation or Bureau of Services for the Visually Impaired, at:

14650 Detroit Ave., Suite 300　　Fax: (216) 227-3293
Lakewood, OH 44107-4210　　　Toll-free: 1-866-325-0026
Ph: (216) 227-3250　　　　　　　TTY: (216) 227-3292

Two Are Better Than One
▪ How to Accept Help When You Need It ▪

Your life circumstances can change in an instant. And when they do, friends and family may want to lighten your load as you navigate bumps in the road. The assistance that they provide can help you concentrate on what's truly important at this particular time in your life. This may mean that you need help while dealing with a medical emergency, adoption, birth of a child, illness, death in the family, or divorce.

On the other side of the coin, you may find yourself needing help orchestrating a big project like a wedding, fundraiser, or writing a book. All of these are reasons to graciously accept help when it is offered. Why? Because you cannot attend to the situation at hand and continue life as usual. You need more than just your own two hands to cope with your situation. Therefore, this is not a time to let your pride hold you back from doing everything you must do. Simply put: You need to accept the help of others to survive and to get through this time in your life. So, don't be a fool and turn down help when it's offered.

Accepting help is not a sign of weakness. Rather, it is indeed a sign that you clearly understand the needs of the situation and you are preparing to meet them. The Bible tells us, in Ecclesiastes 4:9, that two people are better off than one, for they can help each other succeed. Your goal is to succeed. Your goal now is to see that you or your family member gets better and the children get fed.

Accepting help means you need to:

1. Realize the situation is too big for you to deal with by yourself.

2. Get a hold of your emotions by praying and asking God for guidance and wisdom. You may also want to do some deep breathing, and then begin to speak all the positive words you can think of each and every day to carry you through the stressful situation.

3. Make a list of your immediate needs (today and tomorrow).

4. Contact by phone, text, e-mail, or blackberry your friends, family, and/or church for immediate assistance.

Two Are Better Than One
• How to Accept Help When You Need It •

5. Make a list of your essential needs for the next week as the situation requires.

6. Contact those who have expressed a desire to help you (if needed).

After the first couple of days, you will probably need to access the situation again. And above all else, you will also need to remember to take good care of yourself. That means you need to eat, get some rest, and try to take a walk or exercise to help reduce your stress.

All these things will help keep you strong so you are able to make good decisions, avoid illness and fatigue, and have the physical and mental stamina to encourage those around you who need it. Sometimes it may take a while for your loved ones and family members to heal and overcome the situation at hand. Be patient with them and also with yourself.

If You Need More Help: If you find your situation is still uncertain, but you realize you need more help, read the information below on further accessing your needs.

Further Accessing Your Needs: What do you say when someone offers to help you, but you aren't sure yet of what you need?

During times of crisis, decisions are made as life unfolds moment by moment. When you aren't sure of what you need, the first thing to do is ask for the person's phone number – and tell them, "I appreciate your offer to help. Right now however, I am not sure exactly what kind of help I need. Can I get back to you when I have a better idea of how you can help me?" (Advice from Lee Woodruff, wife of ABC newsman Bob Woodruff after her husband's traumatic brain injury, on ABC's television show, *The View.*)

See Appendix E for a list of items you may need help with.

Workspace: Record More Information Here
~ Healing ~

Healing: Healing can come over a long period of time or in an instant. It can come through physical therapy, surgery, medication, counseling, saying "no" more often, changing your lifestyle, or embracing a mind-set that does not allow for self-pity or giving up. It can also come as a result of praise and prayer.

Healing and Your Life: In order to lead a productive, joyful, and healthy life, you need to be freed up from your past. Then and only then will you be fully available to partake of the opportunities and possibilities that present themselves today.

Record Ways to Become a Healthier You: Record below the specific healing you need in your life. Are you angry or bitter? Do you need to forgive someone? Are you in any emotional, spiritual, or physical pain? Are you experiencing any distress at home? Record below specifc ideas and actions you will take to make your life better.

Wisdom is choosing right now what you'll be satisfied with later on.
– *Joyce Meyer, Christian teacher and speaker, on her TV show,* Enjoying Everyday Life

Feeling Overwhelmed? Here's a great tip that only calls for a piece of paper and a pen. This technique will make your life so much easier and better! It will remove the "overwhelm" and help you begin to take action.

Ready, Set, Go!

1. Take a pad of paper and divide it into four quarters. In the top left section write "ASAP"

2. In the top right section write "this week"

3. In the bottom left section write "in the next 30 days"

4. In the bottom right section write "future"

5. Now, begin going through all your scraps of paper with "to-do" items written on them, and begin plugging these projects into one of the sections on your pad.

6. Lastly, sort through all of the ideas swimming around in your mind that you have not yet captured on paper and write them down in the appropriate quadrant.

This simple exercise will free up your mind and allow you to be productive, organized, and in control. (Thanks to D'vorah Lansky, M.Ed., Bestselling Author and Marketing Wizard --http://BookMarketingMadeEasy.com)

To get to point D where you ultimately want to be, you must pass through points A, B, and C. Those places hold valuable experiences that you'll need for wherever you're going in life. *– Nanci J. Gravill, Author of Fresh Hope ... Cleveland*

When you're tired of
all the waves
in life...

Classes For You!

Classes and Seminars to Help You and Your Family

All of the local churches below provide Biblically-based, Christian growth classes for individuals of all ages. These classes can help you to heal and to move forward in life. Some may also provide referrals to local Christian counselors and psychologists. Be whole, be happy, be well!

Please Note: This is not a complete list of churches in this area. See Appendix F for addresses and website information on the churches below.

Churches/Locations:

- Christ Church (Columbia Station/Strongsville border)
  Groups / classes offered: B C J M N W S W FF JJ

- Christ the King Church (North Olmsted)
  Groups / classes offered: B S LL

- Church on the Rise (Westlake)
  Groups / classes offered: B N Z

- Cuyahoga Valley Church (Broadview Heights)
  Groups / classes offered: A B K N X Q S Y Z DD GG HH

- Grace Church (Middleburg Heights)
  Groups / classes offered: A B N V X CC

- Mt. Zion Church (Oakwood Village)
  Groups / classes offered: B J S V DD KK GG

- North Olmsted Evangelical Friends Church (North Olmsted)
  Groups / classes offered: B E F H N Q R U X

- Parkside Church (Solon / Chagrin Falls)
  Groups / classes offered: B J N R S V Y Z GG AA DD II

- Royal Redeemer Lutheran Church (North Royalton)
  Groups / classes offered: B C K L N AA CC EE FF II

- The Word Church (Greater Cleveland/ Warrensville Heights)
  Groups / classes offered: A D E F G H I T U Z GG II

Classes and Seminars to Help You and Your Family (continued)

Classes & Seminars Key

A.   Abortion & Miscarriage Healing & Care

B.   Addiction Recovery / Support

C.   Alcoholics Anonymous

D.   Anger Management (Youth & Adult)

E.   Betrayed Hearts (Healing from the husband's sexual betrayal in marriage)

F.   (Women): Boundaries (Learning how to say "no")

G.   (Women): Breaking the Silence (Emotional, physical, and mental abuse)

H.   (Women): Healing the Father/Mother Wounds (Father hurts / wounds)

I.   (Women): Safe People: Learning How to Identify and Move into Safe Relationships

J.   Cancer Care / Support

K.   Care / Encouragement Ministry

L.   Caring for Aging Parents

M.   Choosing Forgiveness

N.   Divorce Care/ Recovery

O.   Divorce Care for Kids

P.   Domestic Violence and Abusive Relationships

Q.   Eating Disorders Care Group

R.   Embracing Family (Adoption)

S.   Grief Counseling / Ministry

T.   Grief Recovery for Teens

U.   Homosexuality Issues (men's only and women's only)

V.   Job Seekers Network

W.   Life Hurts – God Heals - Students with Pain and Addiction

X.   Making Peace – Helping Resolve Past Issues & Move Towards Growth

Y.   Managing Your Money

Z.   Marriage

AA. Parenting

AB. Parenting – Single Parent Ministry

AC. Prayer Ministry

Classes and Seminars to Help You and Your Family (continued)

AD. Pre-Marital Counseling

AE. Promise Keepers (Men)

AF. Reaching the Heart of Your Teen

AG. Relationship and Sex Addictions (men's only / women's only)

AH. Sexual Abuse Recovery

AI.   SOS Ministry: Seasons of Singleness

AJ. Traumatic Brain Injury and Stroke

AK. Wealth Ministry

AL. Women's Mental Health Support Group

ALSO: Financial Peace University - Dave Ramsey's Money Management Classes
Please see www.daveramsey.com for classes in your community.

Workspace: Record Helpful Ideas Here
~ Embrace Healthy Emotions and Relationships ~

Complete, Lacking Nothing: God's goal is that we become whole and complete individuals in Christ. Therefore, let go of wrong thinking and negative feelings that don't serve your life well. Get rid of bitterness and anger. Forgive. God is waiting to help you let go.

Record Ways to Embrace Healing and Move Forward in Life: Record below any risks you may need to take in order to embrace wholeness. This may mean making a phone call and asking for forgiveness or choosing to let go of your anger and make peace with your childhood and your parents.

Record Ways to Embrace More of Today: The past is simply that, the past. Are you clinging to any habits, ideas, or ways of thinking that keep you from moving forward in life? For example, you may be holding onto the idea that you will only accept a job with a starting time of 9 a.m. Holding on to that idea would make it harder for you to get a job. How can you be more flexible? What ideas can you let go of? Take a few minutes to reflect and then record that information here.

If you so cling to the past, you'll never embrace your future.
– *Nanci J. Gravill, Author of Fresh Hope ... Cleveland*

Record Ideas to Help You Enjoy Your Life: Is there anything you've been wanting to do – take a vacation, become a gourmet cook, or write a book? Record those ideas here. Record also any obstacles to achieving those goals.

Record Other Thoughts: You may want to use the space below to record your feelings or your thoughts about how your life is unfolding today.

Do not look back and grieve over the past for it is gone; and do not be troubled about the future, for it has not yet come. Live in the present, and make it so beautiful it will be worth remembering. – *Author unknown*[48]

Record Anything That Comes to Your Mind Here. This is a good place to reflect, dream, give thanks, spill out your heart, or gather your thoughts. This space may also provide a great place for you to brainstorm.

Life is full of lots of or ordinary days. It's what you do with them that counts!
– *Nanci J. Gravill, Author of Fresh Hope … Cleveland*

The intelligent man

is always

open to new ideas.

In fact, he looks for them.

–The Living Bible (Proverbs 18:15)

Internet Safety

1. FBI PUBLICATIONS: A PARENT'S GUIDE TO INTERNET SAFETY

   As its website shares, from the FBI: "Dear
   Parent: Our children are our Nation's most valuable asset."
   Website: www.fbi.gov/publications/pguide/pguidee.htm

2. KID SAFETY on the INTERNET - The Police Notebook

   Per their webslte, Kid Safety is "a law enforcement site promoting safety and crime prevention for kids." The site reviews all the necessary safety issues and explains what to do in cases of emergency.

   Website: www.ou.edu/oupd/kidsafe/start.htm

3. SOCIAL MEDIA SITES: Social media sites are Internet sites used specifically for social interactions, like Facebook, Twitter, and LinkedIn, to name just a few.

   Both articles, "Please Rob Me" and "5 Security Dangers" (below), have been reprinted from *The Publicity Hound's Tips of the Week*, an e-zine (online magazine) featuring tips, tricks and tools for generating free publicity.[49] Subscribe at www.publicityhound.com, and receive by e-mail the handy cheat sheet, "89 Reasons to Send a Press Release."

   ~ PLEASE ROB ME ~ Do you broadcast when you're leaving your home or office? Lots of people do. And every day, their avatars and "here's where I am now" messages are showing up at www.pleaserobme.com, a site that mocks them for announcing to the world they're not home and actually makes it easier for burglars to rob them.

   You put yourself at risk when you use www.foursquare.com, a social media site that makes it easy to "check in" with your friends, in conjunction with blasting out those messages to your Twitter and Facebook friends.

   Find out how it works and what you can do to keep yourself from showing up on this site. Visit www.publicityhound.net, where Joan Stewart, a publicity hound, writes about it in her blog.

SOCIAL MEDIA SITES (*continued*)

~ 5 Security Dangers ~

If you're on Facebook, LinkedIn, or MySpace, *Consumer Reports* says you're putting your security at risk if you do these five things:

1. List your correct birthday.

2. Use a weak password.

3. Overlook the control you have over your privacy settings.

4. Post a child's name in a caption.

5. Mention being away from home.

Read about two other social media dangers in the L.A. Times blog. See their article from May 3, 2010, via the following link: www.latimesblogs.latimes.com/technology/2010/05/internet-security-what-not-to-post-on-facebook

PARENTAL CONTROL SOFTWARE: SAFE EYES

Parental Control Software, or Safe Eyes, protects children online by blocking pornography, filtering YouTube content and online TV, and monitoring social networking (Facebook, chat, etc.). Works on up to three computers in one household. Financial guru Dave Ramsey has endorsed this software. (Also listed under Emergency Numbers, p. 83.)

Website: http://x3watch.com/safeeyes.html

Internet Suggestions: Take a minute today to check your Internet settings. You may only want your closest friends to have access to your information.

There's Value in Interacting with Others: You can learn so much from other people. Face-to-face contact gives you a chance to improve your communication skills, helps build confidence in a variety of situations, and prepares you to deal with others in the workforce. Besides that, online relationships don't allow you to hear a person's voice or receive a big old hug if you need one. If you spend 30 minutes on Facebook and LinkedIn, make sure you also spend 30 minutes in face-to-face contact with a real, live person! Don't sit behind a computer all day!

Record Ways to Increase Your Face-to Face Interactions: Record practical ways to move from sitting behind your computer to interacting and finding out more about others.

Twitter is a great place to tell the world what you're thinking before you've had a chance to think about it. – *Chris Pirillo, blogger (b. 1973)* [50]

Books open your mind,
broaden your mind,
and
strengthen you
as nothing else can.

William Feather, (1889 – 1981), *Cleveland Press* reporter,
Cleveland, Ohio, businessman, and editor [51]

Check Out These

BOOKS

Books are great resources. They can provide encouragement, give you new ideas, show you how to do things, and help you improve in many ways!

Suggestion: Whenever you hear of a good book via the television or at the library, write the title on a 3 x 5" index card. Then place the card in a file box for safekeeping. When you have time and are looking for a good book, you can just reach into your file box and choose the one you'd like to read right now.

Listed on the next two pages are a few books you may want to read, purchase, or at least browse through! There's nothing like a good book!

Health & Well-Being

1. *The Blue Zone: Lessons for Living Longer from the People Who've Lived the Longest* – Dan Buettner ("A must-read if you want to stay young!" -Dr. Oz)

2. *Dr. C. Everett Koop's Self-Care Advisor: Essential Home Health Guide for You and Your Family* – Dr. C. Everett Koop (a great home reference book)

3. *SuperFoods Rx: Fourteen Foods That Will Change Your Life* – Steven Pratt, M.D.

4. *YOU: The Owner's Manual, Updated and Expanded Edition: An Insider's Guide to the Body That Will Make You Healthier and Younger* – Drs. Oz and Roizen

5. *YOU: The Smart Patient: An Insider's Handbook for Getting the Best Treatment* – Drs. Oz and Roizen (how to select the best doctors and surgeons)

Books

Living Better – Living Well

1. *The Battlefield of the Mind* – Joyce Meyer

2. *Embrace Your Second Calling: Find Passion and Purpose For the Rest of You Life (A Woman's Guide)* – Dale Hanson Bourke

3. *The Five Love Languages: How to Express Heartfelt Commitment to Your Mate (Note: Other versions don't include a mate)* – Dr. Gary Chapman

4. *Find Your Strongest Life* – Marcus Buckingham

5. *100 Ways to Simplify Your Life* – Joyce Meyer

6. *Overcoming Crisis: The Secrets to Thriving in Challenging Time*s – Dr. Myles Munroe

7. *The Total Money Makeover* – Dave Ramsey

Strength, Inspiration, and Help from God – (All written by Christians)

1. *Believe That You Can* – Jentezen Franklin

2. *The Me I Want to Be: Becoming God's Best Version of You* – John Ortberg

3. *The Purpose Driven Life* – Rick Warren

4. *The Secret Power of Speaking God's Word* – Joyce Meyer

5. *Your Best Life Now* – Joel Osteen

Workspace: Record Some Good Books
~ Read. Fill Your Heart and Mind with Great Things. ~

Record the Titles of Books You Want to Read: Use this space to record any books or videos you would like to get at the library, bookstore, or online.

Record Other Events: Use this space also to record any lectures or book signings you'd like to attend. Learning new things will keep you young and healthy!

Books are the quietest and most constant of friends; they are the most accessible and wisest of counselors, and the most patient of teachers.
– *Charles W. Eliot, (1869-1909), President of Harvard University* [52]

Life is 10 percent

what happens to you

and

90 percent how you react to it.

– Charles Swindoll, American writer and clergyman (1934 -)[53]

Facing Challenges

We all face challenges. Here are some great tips from the RN Central website article, "100 Positive Thinking Exercises that Will Make Any Patient Healthier and Happier," August 19, 2008.[54] To read more of the article, go to www.rncentral.com/positivethinking.

1. Don't let yourself quit. Giving up is usually taking the easy way out of a situation... You'll thank yourself in the long run if you don't give up.

2. Don't expect change to be easy. No one ever promised that making a big change in your life would be easy...Don't let opposition make you lose your confidence and adopt a negative attitude.

3. Find the bright side. Every cloud has a silver lining...Try finding the bright spot amid all the turmoil surrounding a situation. Focus on that.

4. Understand that the situation is not forever.

5. Truly believe you will succeed...Believe that you will be successful. This may give you the confidence and assurance you need to make the difference.

6. Face up to change. The world and those around you are constantly changing... Make peace with these changes and understand they don't always mean the end of happiness, just because they're something different.

7. Make a conscious decision to be resilient. In life you can either let a challenge break you down and make you see the world in a negative light, or you can draw on strength you didn't even know you had and rise above it. Choose the latter...it's never too late.

8. See the beauty in everything. Even if you're in the worst mood, taking the time to look at all the beautiful things that surround you in the world can provide you with an instant and insightful lift to your spirits.

9. Realize that your thoughts do not own you. Stop your negative thoughts in their tracks by realizing that you're in charge of what you think, not the other way around.

10. Accept the good things. Sometimes we get so caught up in the bad stuff coming our way that we forget to appreciate the good things. Take a minute to sit down and think of all the positive things that happened in your day, no matter how small.

More importantly, get excited about all the possibilities that lie ahead. Even in the midst of the biggest disasters, there are a multitude of possibilities that await you to make changes or to take on the world tomorrow.

There are possibilites ahead!

What Should You Think About? The Bible tells us in Philippians 4:8 what we are to think about. "Summing it all up my friends. I'd say you'll do best by filling your minds and meditating on things true, noble, reputable, authentic, compelling, gracious—the best, not the worst; the beautiful, not the ugly; things to praise, not things to curse." (The Message)

Record Good Things to Think About: You can develop patterns of thinking that will bring about wrong or negative mindsets. So how can you sift your thinking? Shifting your thoughts will take a conscious effort on your part to recognize your thoughts and then direct them to other more positive ones. Record below some positive words, ideas, thoughts, and subject matters that you wish to dwell on.

The happiness of your life depends on the quality of your thoughts.
– *Marcus Aurelius (first-century Roman emperor)*[55]

Record Your Blessings: Often times we focus on the wrong things; when we do, everything can look so much worse. Please use the area below to record all the blessings you can think of in your life.

Record These Things Every Morning: Practice gratefulness each morning. If you are going through a tough time right now, you may want to begin your day by recording five (5) different things that make you feel grateful. Dwell on those things throughout the day. Repeat this practice of looking for five different things every day until you are feeling positively wonderful!

Reflect upon your present blessings, of which every man has plenty;
not on your past misfortunes, of which all men have some.
– *Charles Dickens, (1812 – 1870), English novelist*[56]

Record Your Goals and Dreams: God has not changed. He is still able to work in your life even in difficult times. There is no recession in Heaven. Therefore, you should write out your goals and dreams. In fact, writing them down increases the probability you will actually see those things come to pass.

Record below your goals and any dreams or ideas you may have for your future.

The Lord answered me, and said, Write the vision, and make it plain
upon tables, so he may run that reads it. For the vision is yet for
an appointed time, but at the end it shall speak, and not lie: though
it tarry, wait for it; – King James Bible (Habakkuk 2: 2-3)

Something More

Nobody can go back
and start a new beginning,
but
anyone can start today and
make a new ending.

– Maria Robinson, writer Vermont Studio Center[57]

Reflection

Perhaps by now, you have used some of the information in the previous three sections and you're feeling more encouraged and inspired. As in the others, this section offers you ideas and help to make your life better. But this section offers you a different kind of help and support. It's the kind of help that will last for a lifetime and more.

Described below are some ways that your life might be unfolding right now. Take a quick peek and see if you identify with any one of these scenarios.

• Although you mind your manners but still don't eat your vegetables, you now realize your mother was right • THINGS DO HAPPEN FOR A REASON!

• At the moment, you're feeling adventuresome and you're having a great day • Then again, you're someone who loves life, and you're determined to have a good attitude no matter what • FOR YOU, THE GLASS IS DEFINITELY HALF FULL!

• Maybe you bake raspberry pies and luscious lemon tarts • Your garden is always full of vegetables and herbs • Jumping rope keeps you young • You read the newspaper and frequently visit with your neighbors • Tonight your kids are coming for dinner • Life is good, yet STILL YOU WANT MORE!

• Or perhaps you've never told anyone about your dreams • You want to finish school and open your own business • You really hope your dreams can come true because for you, THERE MUST BE SOMETHING MORE.

• But more than anything, you're reading this "just because" • Because in this universe, there seems to be endless possibilities • How do you tap into that power? COULD THERE BE MORE?

The next several pages contain wisdom and strength for your life. Here you will find the most powerful resource you could ever possess. Please open your heart and your mind before turning the page.

Welcome to a place where you'll find many good things for your life! This section greets you warmly with a promise to help you discover joy and power for living every day!

As we all know, life presents each one of us with challenges. Some of these challenges are minor, yet some decide the entire direction of our lives. And from our own perspective it's often unclear why things happen the way they do. In the book *When Bad Things Happen to Good People*, author Harold S. Kushner expands upon this very idea with help from Thornton Wilder's novel *The Eighth Day*. The conclusion of Wilder's book shares an interesting concept of why good people have to suffer in this life. He says:

> God has a pattern into which all of our lives fit. His pattern requires that some lives be twisted, knotted, or cut short, while others extend to impressive lengths, not because one thread is more deserving than another, but simply because the pattern requires it. Looked at from underneath, from our vantage point in life, God's pattern of reward and punishment seems arbitrary and without design, like the underside of a tapestry. But looked at from outside this life, from God's vantage point, every twist and knot is seen to have its place in a great design that adds up to a work of art.[58]

What a wonderful perspective filled with depth and beauty. Yes, more than anything God does want to make your life a masterpiece. But the only way that God can artfully design the magnificent canvas of your life is if you come to know Him personally. And as you do, graciously allow Him to choose the colors and most fitting design for your life's tapestry.

If you've gone to church but have never heard about knowing God personally and having a personal relationship with Him, please take a comfortable seat and let me tell you about the best friend you could ever have!

God is a warm and caring heavenly Father who is always faithful and loving to His dear children. Yet before the sun, moon, and stars were ever created, God had a purpose for your life. And He thought about you long ago, before He fashioned the intricate details of your character, intellect, and personality. He also designed your physique and decided on the great talents you'd be able to share with the world.

But more than anything, God loves you. And that's precisely why He wants to have a relationship with you. It stands to reason too that if you love someone, you want to spend time with them; you want to nurture that relationship. And because God cares about us so much, He is often sad and hurt by the way we live. You see, He never intended us to be afraid, worried, depressed, angry, or impatient. Instead, God intended us to be joyful and fulfilled in a relationship with Him.

Because He is such a great and awesome God, when you put your trust completely in Him, your life will never be the same. Now, this doesn't mean you won't ever have a problem. But through the valleys and up to the breathtaking mountaintop moments of your life, He will be there to guide, protect, comfort, and strengthen you. And while we as human beings are limited by our own abilities, God has no limitations. Every challenge, concern, and everything else in between can be transformed by His power working in your life. There's nothing too difficult for God!

Today as you're reading this, all you need to do to have this relationship with God is say a little prayer (below). You simply need to invite God's Son, Jesus Christ, to come into your heart. Christ died on the cross for your sins – fear, worry, anger, impatience, pride, living for yourself – the things that keep you separated from a holy God. Religion, philosophy, and good works have always been man's attempt to reach God. Christ's death on the cross was God reaching down to man to bring us back into a relationship with Him, the living God. But Jesus not only died for us; He rose again! And His victory over death means you can have victory in your life, too!

Prayer ~ to Know Christ as Your Savior:

Dear Lord Jesus,

I know that I've done a lot of things wrong, and I ask Your forgiveness. I believe You died on the cross for my sins and rose from the dead. Today I turn from my sins and invite You to come into my heart and life. I want to start trusting and following You as my Lord and Savior. Thank you for my new life in Christ. Amen.

As you live for God, you will experience victory by obeying God's Word, the Bible. To grow in your faith, make sure you find a church where Christ is preached. There you'll meet other believers who will help keep you encouraged. If you prayed the above prayer, welcome to the family of God!

Your Name: Date Christ Came into Your ♥:

I invited Jesus into my heart today. (Write any thoughts here.) †

Therefore if anyone is in Christ, he is a new creation.
The old things have passed away. Behold, all things have become new.
—The New American Standard Bible (II Corinthians 5:17)

Divine Recipe for Living
·· *for good health and success in life* ··

<u>Combine</u>:

1 pinch of *Favor* (Psalms 90:17) ~ pp. 3, 139
1 T. *Peace* (Psalms 29:11) ~ p. xix
2 T. *Trust* (Psalms 4:5b) ~ pp. 51, 52
½ cup of *Faith* (Hebrews 11:1, 6) ~ p. 53
¼ cup of *Humility* (I Peter 5:6) ~ (pride) p. 47
¼ cup of *Obedience* (Proverbs 19:23) ~ (choose to obey) p. 104
1 ¼ cups *Wise Counsel* (Proverbs 15:22) ~ pp. 101 -102, 105
1 ½ cups of *Wisdom* (James 1:5) ~ p. 87, 105

<u>Mix</u>:

1 cup *Positive Words & Thoughts* (Proverbs 18:21a) ~ p. 48, 50
2 T. *Vision for the Future* (Jeremiah 29:11) (classes) ~ pp. 90, 91
½ cup *Hope* (Jeremiah 29:11) ~ pp. viii, xvi, 49, 56
1½ cups *Patience* (Galatians 5:22) ~ pp. xiv, 73
2 cups *Perseverance* (James 1:12) ~ (strength) pp. 11, 105

~~~~~~

Combine favor, peace, trust, faith, humility, obedience, wise counsel, and wisdom.

Mix well the remaining ingredients of positive words and thoughts, vision for the future with eyes fixed on God, hope, patience, and perseverance.

Fold both mixtures together well, and pour into a heart and mind already prepared with God's Word, prayer, and the confidence that you can do it (Numbers 13:30)!

Bake until the mixture has been transformed according to the excellent and perfect will of God for your life (Proverbs 16:9).

Guaranteed: success, peace and blessings!

Last Thoughts

Here are two last thoughts ~ let them empower you!

Thought #1:

The Chinese use two brush strokes to write the word "crisis."
One brush stroke stands for danger; the other for opportunity.
In a crisis, be aware of the danger —but recognize the opportunity.

— John F. Kennedy (35th President of the United States)[59]

Thought #2:

Ten Steps to Success: These steps to success are so inspiring. They were on a banner that was displayed in a middle school classroom where developmentally disabled students were taught. Individuals with disabilities work harder than most of us and are usually the last to give up. When things seem difficult, read these over and try the steps. And above all else, Don't Give Up!

Ten Steps to Success

    10. Just keep trying.
    9. Try to determine what is working.
    8. Try to determine what is NOT working.
    7. Try to find someone who has done it.
    6. Try and ask for help.
    5. Try it again tomorrow.
    4. Try it again a little differently.
    3. Try once more.
    2. Try again.
    1. TRY!

This is the only life you get: make it a good one.
God bless you!
— Nanci

Last Thoughts

God is the only one who can make the valley of trouble a door of hope.
– Catherine Marshall, (1914 – 1983), American author [60]

To enjoy a life filled with peace, strength, stability, and success no matter what the circumstances, requires taking small steps every day toward your goal. And if you don't give up, at the right time the doors that were once closed will swing wide open for you. Behind those doors, of course, lie all your hopes, dreams, and every other good thing that God so wants to give you.

Today, seize every opportunity to do good. Desire excellence for your life. Say your prayers and expect them to be answered in a miraculous way, because not only does God love you, but He is able to do exceedingly, abundantly beyond all that we could ask, think, or even imagine (Ephesians 3:20). God is not only able to do the miraculous in your life – He WANTS to!

❖

God is not only able
to do
the miraculous
in
your life –
He wants to!

❖

Appendices

Appendix A
50-Plus Shopper Perks & AAA Discounts

Aurora Farms Premium Outlets

This early-American style village was once a market selling primarily meats, fruits, and vegetables. Now, as an outlet mall, shoppers can purchase merchandise from its 70 designer and name-brand outlet stores. Shoppers can choose quality merchandise at factory-direct savings of twenty-five to sixty-five percent.

- ❖ Discounts: Shoppers age fifty and older receive ten percent off their entire purchase every Tuesday at select stores. Visit the Information Center for a list of participating stores. Proof of age may be required at the time of purchase. Cannot be combined with any other coupon, sale or promotion.

- ❖ Other Offers: Other sidewalk sales are offered throughout the year. Check their website for more details.

- ❖ Coupons: Two VIP coupons are available on the outlets' website. Print these coupons and then present them at the outlets' information center. You'll then receive FREE VIP coupon books with additional discounts at participating stores.

Address:

549 South Chillicothe Rd (Route 43) ▪ Aurora, Ohio 44202

(near Geauga Lake's Wildwater Kingdom)

Ph: (330) 562-2000

Website: www.premiumoutlets.com

American Automobile Association (AAA)

If you have an AAA membership, you can take advantage of many discounts and savings. Visit www.aaa.com, fill in your zip code, and click on the "discount" tab to find all kinds of member discounts. Simply show your card to save on many services, retailers, and restaurants, including Dell Computer, computer services at Geek Squad (in Best Buy), prescriptions from CVS and Caremark, the Hard Rock Café, Marriott and Hyatt Hotels, plus many other stores, theaters, museums, and entertainment discounts!

Appendix B
Beauty/Grooming

To look and feel your best, contact the beauty schools below for more on hours of operation, prices, and services available.

1. Cuyahoga Valley Career Center ~ Ph: (440) 526-5200
   8001 Brecksville Road (Route 21), Brecksville, Ohio 44141

2. Grace College of Cosmetology ~ Ph: (440) 843-8810
   13377 Smith Road, Middleburg Heights, Ohio 44130

3. Polaris's New Beginnings Salon ~ Ph: (440) 891-7875
   7285 Old Oak Boulevard, Middleburg Heights, Ohio 44130
   The salon is inside Polaris Career Center.

4. Cisoria Academy of Cosmetology ~ Ph: (216) 475-3535
   20880 Southgate Park Boulevard, Maple Heights, Ohio 44137

5. The Cut Beauty School ~ Ph: (216) 320-1444
   13238 Cedar Road, Cleveland Heights, Ohio 44118

6. Fairview Academy O & D Beauty, Inc. ~ Ph: (440) 734-5555
   22610 Lorain Avenue, Fairview Park, Ohio 44126

7. Inner State Beauty School ~ Ph: (440) 461-1000
   5150 Mayfield Road, Lyndhurst, Ohio 44124

8. Lake Erie Barber College ~ Ph: (216) 391-5322
   2234 East 55th Street, Cleveland, Ohio 44103

9. Paul Mitchell – The Ohio Academy ~ Ph: (330) 963-0119
   10735 Ravenna Road, Twinsburg, Ohio 44087

10. Normandy High School Cosmetology Clinic ~ Ph: (440) 885-8393
    2500 W. Pleasant Valley Road, Parma, Ohio 44134

11. Raphael's School of Beauty ~ Ph: (440) 716-8153
    24761 Lorain Avenue, North Olmsted, Ohio 44070

Appendix C
Contacts for Job Search Groups

- Bay United Methodist Church in Bay Village (440) 871-2082
  Contact: Reverend William Buckeye, bayumc@sbcglobal.net

- Fairmount Presbyterian Church in Cleveland Heights (216) 321-5800
  Contact: Tom Johnston, (216) 789-9850, tj@searchpath.com
  (Careers in Transition)

- Grace Church in Middleburg Heights (440) 243-4885
  Contact: Jim Jasko, (216) 267-4300, jjjasko@gmail.com

- Parkside Church in Bainbridge/Solon (440) 543-1212
  Career Connections, www.parksidechurch.com/ministries/support-workshops
  Contact: Dan Larison, dlarison@parksidechurch.com

- Pioneer Memorial Presbyterian Church in Solon (440) 248-4756
  Chagrin Valley Job Seekers Group (CVJS)
  Contact: Jim Grant, (440) 248-6042, jwgrant@aol.com
  Greg Reynolds, (440) 248-2181, cvjsgreg@yahoo.com

- St. Albert the Great Catholic Church in North Royalton (440) 237-6760
  Contact: Lorie Milano, lmilano33@sbcglobal.net

- St. Basil Catholic Church in Brecksville (440) 526-1686
  http://www.basilthegreat.org/job_support/index.asp

- St. Paul's Episcopal Church in Cleveland Heights (216) 932-5815
  Contact: Jamie Hogg, (216) 991-6799

Other Employment Resources

- Employment Connection (Cuyahoga County Re-employment Service Center)
  11699 Brookpark Road, Parma
  Ph: (216) 898-1366 ~ Free services and classes for the unemployed.

- The Career Center, Maple Heights Branch Library
  Ph: (216) 475-2225 ~ Career counselors, career assessment tests, and
  workshops. Counselors and workshops travel to various library locations.

Appendix D
Bakery Outlet Locations

Entenmann's
5702 Mayfield Road
Lyndhurst, OH 44124
(440) 449-0866

8367 Pearl Road
Strongsville, OH 44136
(440) 891-8463

Wonder/Hostess
6277 Pearl Road
Parma Heights, OH 44130
(440) 845-9200

Schwebel's
9701 Walford Avenue
Cleveland, OH 44102
(216) 651-6200

345 East 200th Street
Euclid, OH 44119
(216) 481-1880

22626 Royalton Road
Strongsville, OH 44136
(440) 846-1921

Appendix E

Two Are Better than One

▪ How to accept help when you need it ▪

While life circumstances may never be easy to endure, the list of things below could be a great place to start accessing your immediate needs as you navigate through your challenges.

You may need help to do the following:

___ Apply for Family Medical Leave with employer

___ Help with holiday meals / shopping

___ Buy gifts for helpful friend or medical staff

___ Grocery shopping

___ Childcare / Pick up children

___ Lifting / carrying items at home

___ Cleaning/washing/packing

___ Make phone calls

___ Contact friends and family

___ Pay medical bills and file claims

___ Contact pastor, priest, or rabbi

___ Pick up / deliver items from home

___ Feed children

___ Respite care (see insurance benefits)

___ Feed pet(s)

___ Ride to church or Bible study

___ Fix Meals / Deliver Meals

___ Ride to doctors, hospital, or therapy

___ Lunch with a caring friend

___ Run errands

___ Visit doctor (support/help with medical info)

___ Stay overnight -aging parent or child

___ Let in scheduled maintenance or cable

___ Water plants, take in mail

Activities of daily living in caring for a loved one: *See Glossary.*

See your health care benefits regarding: home health aide, hospice, respite care.

Appendix F
Church Addresses & Information

NOTE: The "healing" classes featured in Part III, *More Fresh Hope Resources*, are usually offered at the larger Bible-based churches, such as those below. Please check each church's website for a more complete list of classes, programs, and worship times.

- Christ Church (Columbia Station) – www.christchurchohio.org
  23080 Royalton Road (at Strongsville border); Ph: 440-236-8282

- Christ the King Church (North Olmsted) – www.ctkchurch.org
  30635 Lorain Avenue; Ph: 440-777-3333

- Church on the Rise (Westlake) – www.churchonetherise.net
  3550 Crocker Road; Ph: 440-808-0200

- Cuyahoga Valley Church (Broadview Heights) – www.cvconline.org
  5055 Wallings Road; Ph: 440-746-0404

- Grace Church (Middleburg Heights) – www.gracecma.org
  7393 Pearl Road; Ph: 440-243-4885

- Mt. Zion Church (Oakwood Village) – http://mtzionoakwood.org/
  One Mount Zion Circle; Ph: (440) 232-2645

- North Olmsted Evangelical Friends Church (North Olmsted) – www.noefc.org
  5665 Great Northern Boulevard; Ph: (440) 779-9484

- Parkside Church (Solon / Chagrin Falls) – www.parksidechurch.com
  7100 Pettibone Road; Ph: 440-543-1212

- Royal Redeemer Lutheran Church (N. Royalton) – www.royred.org
  11680 Royalton Road; Ph: 440-237-7958

- The Word Church (Greater Cleveland / Warrensville Heights) – www.wordcity.org/
  18909 South Miles Road; Ph: 216-332-9673
  North: 2439 East 55th Street, Cleveland
  East: 15320 Euclid Avenue, East Cleveland

Appendix G
The Hospitals of Northeast Ohio

Independent Hospitals

❖ Parma Community General Hospital
7007 Powers Boulevard
Parma, Ohio 44129 – Ph: (440) 743-3000
www.parmahospital.org

❖ Southwest General Health Center (partnered with University Hospitals)
18660 East Bagley Road
Middleburg Heights, Ohio 44130 – Ph: (440) 243-2100
www.swgeneral.com

Center of Excellence & Teaching Hospital Systems

❖ The Cleveland Clinic Foundation (Main Campus)
9500 Euclid Ave.
Cleveland, Ohio 44106 – Ph: (216) 444-2200
www.clevelandclinic.org

Cleveland Clinic Network Hospitals:

Euclid Hospital ~ 18901 Lake Shore Boulevard, Cleveland, 44119 – Ph: (216) 531-9000
Fairview Hospital ~ 18101 Lorain Avenue, Cleveland, 44111 – Ph: (216) 476-7000
Hillcrest Hospital ~ 6780 Mayfield Road, Cleveland, 44124 – Ph: (216) 312-4500
Huron Hospital ~ 13951 Terrace Road, East Cleveland, 44112 – Ph: (216) 761-3300
Lakewood Hospital ~ 14519 Detroit Avenue, Lakewood, 44107 – Ph: (216) 521-4200
Lutheran Hospital ~ 1730 West 25th Street, Cleveland, 44113 – Ph: (216) 696-4300
Marymount Hospital ~ 12300 McCracken Road, Garfield Heights, 44125– Ph: (216) 581-0500
South Pointe Hospital ~ 4110 Warrensville Center Road, Beachwood, 44122 – Ph: (216) 491-6 000

The Hospitals of Northeast Ohio (continued)

<u>The Cleveland Clinic Foundation Family Health Centers (Cuyahoga County only):</u>

Beachwood ~ 26900 Cedar Road, Beachwood, 44122, – Ph: (216) 839-3000

Chagrin Falls ~ 551 East Washington Street, Chagrin Falls, 44022 – Ph: 440-893-9393

East Cleveland ~ 13944 Euclid Avenue, East Cleveland, 44112 – Ph: (216) 767-4242

Independence ~ 5001 Rockside Road, Independence, 44131 – Ph: (216) 986-4000

Lakewood ~ 16215 Madison Avenue, Lakewood, 44107 – Ph: (216) 521-4400

Solon ~ 29800 Bainbridge Road, Solon, 44139 – Ph: (440) 519-6800

Strongsville ~ 16761 South Park Center, Strongsville, 44136 – Ph: (440) 878-2500

Westlake ~ 30033 Clemens Road, Westlake, 44145 – Ph: (440) 899-5555

Teaching Hospital Systems

❖ The MetroHealth System (Main Campus)
   2500 MetroHealth Drive
   Cleveland, 44109 – Ph: (216) 778-7800 ~ www.metrohealth.org

<u>MetroHealth Satellite Offices (Cuyahoga County only):</u>

J. Glenn Smith Health Ctr. ~ 11100 Saint Clair Ave., Cleveland, 44108 – Ph: (216) 249-3600

Asia Plaza Health Ctr. ~ 2999 Payne Ave., Cleveland, 44114 – Ph: (216) 861-4646

Broadway Health Ctr. ~ 6835 Broadway Ave., Cleveland, 44105 – Ph: (216) 957-1500

Brooklyn Medical Group ~ 5208 Memphis Ave., Cleveland, 44144 – Ph: (216) 398-0100

Buckeye Health Ctr. ~ 2816 East 116th St., Cleveland, 44120 – Ph: (216) 957-4000

The Courtlands ~ 29125 Chagrin Blvd., Beachwood, 44122 – Ph: (216) 591-0523

Lee-Harvard Health Ctr. ~ 4071 Lee Rd., Cleveland, 44128 – Ph: (216) 957-1200

Thomas F. McCafferty Health Ctr. ~ 4242 Lorain Ave., Cleveland, 44113 – Ph: (216) 651-5005

Park East ~ 3609 Park East Drive, Beachwood, 44122 – Ph: (216) 957-9959

Strongsville Medical Group ~ 16000 Pearl Rd., Strongsville, 44136 – Ph: (440) 238-2124

Premier Center Westlake ~ 25200 Center Ridge Rd., Westlake, 44145 – Ph: (216) 778-7800

West Park Medical Building ~ 3838 W. 150th St., Cleveland, 44111 – Ph: (216) 957-5000

Appendix G
The Hospitals of Northeast Ohio (continued)

❖ University Hospitals of Cleveland (Main Campus)

    Case Medical Center ▪ Ireland Cancer Center

    MacDonald Women's Hospital ▪ Rainbow Babies & Children's Hospital

    11100 Euclid Ave. Cleveland, 44106 ~ Ph: (866) 844-2273 – www.uhhospitals.org

University Hospitals Satellite Offices (Cuyahoga County only):

Ahuja Medical Center ~ Chagrin Highlands, Beachwood, 44122 – Ph: (216) 593-5500

Bedford Medical Center ~ 44 Blaine Avenue, Bedford, 44146 – Ph: (440) 735-3900

Case Medical Center ~ at University Circle, Cleveland, 44106 – Ph: (216) 844-8447

Chagrin Highlands ~ 3909 Orange Place Ext.*, Orange Village, 44122 – Ph: (216) 896-1700

Chesterland Health Center ~ 8228 Mayfield Road, Chesterland, 44024 – Ph: (440) 729-3200

Euclid Health Center ~ 18599 Lake Shore Boulevard, Cleveland, 44119 – Ph: (216) 383-8500

Landerbrook Health Center ~ 5850 Landerbrook Dr., Cleveland, 44124 – Ph: (440) 646-2626

Mayfield Village Health Ctr. ~ 730 SOM Ctr. Rd., Mayfield Hts., 44143 – Ph: (866) 844-2273

Otis Moss Jr. Health Center ~ 8819 Quincy Avenue, Cleveland, 44106 – Ph: (216) 721-2177

Richmond Medical Ctr. ~ 27100 Chardon Road, Richmond Hts., 44143 – Ph: (440) 585-6500

St. John West Shore ~ 29000 Center Ridge Road, Westlake, 44145 – Ph: (440) 835-8000

University Suburban Health Ctr. ~ 1611 S. Green Rd., S. Euclid, 44121 – Ph: (216) 382-9492

Westlake Health Center ~ 960 Clague Road, Westlake, 44145 – Ph: (440) 250-2100

*Orange Place Extension

Notes

1. Emily Dickinson, " 'Hope' is the thing with feathers--", in *Final Harvest: Emily Dickinson's Poems,* Thomas H. Johnson, ed. Boston: Little, Brown & Company, 1961, 34.
2. *Taber's Cyclopedic Medical Dictionary*, 17th ed., s.v. "Coping skill."
3. Michael Michalko, "Thinking Like a Genius: Eight Strategies Used by the Supercreative, from Aristotle and Leonardo to Einstein and Edison," *The Futurist*, May 1998, p. 21-25.
4. Kevin, Kay Marie Brennfleck, "The Christian Career Center Newsletter," February 26, 2009.
5. Quotegarden.com, accessed August 14, 2011, http://www.qotegarden.com/shopping.html
6. S. W. Straus, ThriftCultureNow.com, accessed January, 27, 2011, http://www.thriftculturenow.com/thrifty-quotes/499-thrift-its-all-in-your-head.
7. Jeff Yeager, As heard on Good Morning America, January 2009
8. John P. Foppe *What's Your Excuse? Making the Most of What You Have.* Christian-career.com, accessed February 2009, http://www.christian-career.com/
9. Memo from Patricia Coyne at the Cuyahoga Valley Career Center, December 29, 2008.
10. Paul Meshanko, "Learning to Manage Time," Pflaum, Bryan,
11. Judy, Stringer, "Your Job Hunt," Cleveland.com.
12. Thinkexist.com, accessed July 15, 2011, http://thinkexist.com/quotations.
13. Thinkexist.com, accessed July 15, 2011, http://thinkexist.com/quotations.
14. The Quote Garden, accessed July 15, 2011, http://quotegarden.com.
15. Brainyquote.com, accessed August 15, 2011, http://brainyquote.com/quotes/authors/b/bob_hope.html
16. Encyclopedia Britannica website, accessed March 13, 2011 URL.
17. Great-Quotes.com, accessed April 14, 2011, www.great-quotes.com/quotes/Audrey/Hepburn.
18. Thinkexist.com, March 12, 2011, http://thinkexist.com/quotations
19. Christian-quotes.com, accessed August 13, 2011, http://christian- quotes.ochristian.com/christian-quotes_ochristian.cgi?find=Christian-quote

Notes

20. Thinkexist.com, accessed August 13, 2011, http://thinkexist.com/quotes/with/keyword/well-being

21. Joel Osteen, *Your Best Life Now: 7 Steps to Living Your Full Potential*, New York: Warner Faith, 2007, p. 122.

22. Joyce Meyer, *Life In the Word* (TV Program), July 3, 2003.

23. Creflo Dollar, *Creflo Dollar Ministries website*, accessed May 1, 2011, www.store.creflodollarministries.org/p-4223-the-power-of-speaking-gods-word.aspx.

24. Joel Osteen, *Your Best Life Now: 7 Steps to Living Your Full Potential*, New York: Faith Words, 2007, p. 122.

25. Elko, Kevin, and Robert L. Shook. *The Pep Talk*. Nashville: Thomas Nelson, 2008

26. "60,000 Quotes".com, accessed July 16, 2011, www.MyFamousQuotes.com

27. Lois Guarino, *Writing Your Authentic Self*, New York: Dell Publishing,1999, p. 18.

28. Joyce Meyer, *Enjoying Everyday Life* (TV show) October 6, 2011.

29. Sarah Ban Breathnach, *Simple Abundance*, New York: Grand Central Publishing, 2005, February18 entry.

30. Susan Jeffers, *Feel the Fear and Do It Anyway*, New York: Hay House CD Audio Books, 2007.

31. University Hospitals, "Maximize Your Memory"; Dr. Daniel Amen's, *Change Your Brain,Change Your Life*, New York: Three Rivers Press, 1998. Heard on public TV, January 2009.

32. www.newsnet5.com/lees5things/18602728/detail.html, accessed on February 3, 2009.

33. Joel Osteen, *Today's Word with Joel Osteen (Devotional)*, June 14, 2011.

34. Thinkexist.com, accessed July 14, 2011, http://thinkexist.com/quotes/mary_anne_radmacher/

35. Joyce Meyer, *Enjoying Everyday Life* (TV show) April 26, 2011.

36. Thinkexist.com, accessed May 11, 2011, http://thinkexist.com/quotations

37. Goodreads website, accessed May 11, 2011, www.goodreads.com/joyce_meyer.

38. *Finding Nemo*, directed by Andrew Stanton and Lee Unkrich, Walt Disney Pictures, 2003.

39. Thinkexist.com, accessed March 12, 2011, http://thinkexist.com/quotation.

40. Thinkexist.com, accessed February 7, 2011, http://thinkexist.com/quotations

Notes

41. Christian Prayer Quotes Assessed September 29, 2011. http://www.christian-prayer-quotes.christian-attorney.net/

42. Fresh Hope Cleveland Blog, assessed October 8, 2011, May 5, 2010 post: Meet Emma. nancigravill.wordpress.com

43. Thinkexist.com, March 12, 2011 and July 16, 2011, http://thinkexist.com/quotatations.com

44. Goodreads website, accessed May 12, 2011, www.goodreads.com/mothertheresa

45. Thinkexist.com, accessed October 10, 2010, http://thinkexist.com/quotations

46. The Quotations Page, accessed May 5, 2011, www.quotatlonspage.com/quote/25870.html

47. Thinkexist.com , accessed September 29, 2011, http://thinkexist.com/quotations/health/

48. Thinkexist.com, accessed May 5, 2011, http://thinkexist.com/quotations

49. Joan Stewart, "The Publicity Hound's Tips of the Week," The Publicity Hound website, accessed February 23, 2010, www.publicityhound.com.

50. Mirna Bard, *Hype-Free Strategy Consultant for Today's Innovators*, under "99 Favorite Social Media Quotes," accessed April 14, 2011, http://www.mirnabard.com/2010/~ 99 Favorite Social Media Quotes.

51. Thinkexist.com, assessed August 11, 2011, http://thinkexist.com/quotations/books

52. Thinkexist.com, accessed July 16, 2011, http://thinkexist.com/quotations.

53. Thinkexist.com, accessed May 11, 2011, www.thinkexist.com/quotations/life.com.

54. RN Central.com, "100 Positive-Thinking Exercises That Will Make Any Patient Healthier and Happier," accessed October 27, 2010, www.rncentral.com/positivethinking.

55. Brainy Quote, accessed May 10, 2011, http://www.brainyquote.com/m/marcus_aurelius_3.html.

56. Brainy Quote, January 28, 2011, http://www.brainyquote.com/quotes/authors/c/charles_dickens_2.html.

57. Thinkexist.com, accessed August 11, 2011, http://thinkexist.com/quotations/life/

58. Harold S. Kushner, *When Bad Things Happen to Good People*, New York: Quill, 2001., p. 18.

59. The Quotations Page, accessed May 10, 2011, www.quotationspage.com/quote/2750.html.

Notes

60. Beliefnet.com, accessed October 8, 2011, www.beliefnet.com/Faiths/Christianity/2009/01/Hope-Quotes-from-Christian-Leader

61. Sanford Health website, accessed April 12, 2011, http://www.sanfordhealth.org/.

Glossary

Activities of Daily Living - Health care professionals and Medicare use this term to access an individual's ability to care for themselves. Activities of daily living are: walking (ambulatory), bathing, dressing/undressing, feeding, toileting, transferring from bed to car and back, and maintaining personal hygiene.

Blog - A blog is a special type of website with frequently updated, journal-like entries. Follow the author's blog, which gives you a behind-the-scenes look at the decisions and concepts behind *Fresh Hope...Cleveland*. New entries are posted every Tuesday and Friday. Visit Nanci's blog anytime at nancigravill.wordpress.com.

Born again – A term that comes from John, 3:3 in the Bible, where Jesus says, "I am telling you the truth: no one can see the Kingdom of God without being born again." When you invite Christ to come into your heart to be your Lord and Savior, you have a new birth, a new life. This term refers to your spiritual birth.

Centers of Excellence – In health care, these are preferred places for care. There, they treat a volume of patients with the same type of illness, and therefore, the staff is better at diagnosing and treating it. In short, they offer patients the most services and deliver the best results.[61]

Facebook – A very popular social networking website introduced in 2004. You can use it to connect with friends and send them messages, as well as promote your events and activities.

Hospice – Both a type of care and a philosophy of care that focuses on providing physical, emotional, and spiritual comfort to terminally ill patients. Services are provided in hospitals, nursing homes, retirement homes, or in the patient's home.

Immune system – A comprehensive system of cells, proteins, tissues, and organs that work together to defend our bodies against germs and microorganisms.

LinkedIn – This social networking website is perfect for making connections for all of your career/professional aspirations. Finding others to join your network can increase your success.

Respite care – A short-term relief program for those who give care at home to an ill family member or friend. Check your health care benefits for coverage of these services.

Bibliography

Amen, Daniel, MD. *Change Your Brain, Change Your Life*. New York: Three Rivers Press, 1998.

Breathnach, Sarah Ban. *Simple Abundance: A Daybook of Comfort and Joy*. New York: Warner Books, 1995.

Brennfleck, Kevin and Kay Marie Brennfleck. *Live Your Calling: A Practical Guide to Finding and Fulfilling Your Mission in Life. San Francisco: Jossey-Bass, 2004*

Dickinson, Emily. " 'Hope' is a thing with feathers." *Final Harvest: Emily Dickinson's Poems.* Thomas H. Johnson, ed. Boston: Little, Brown & Company, 1861.

Elko, Kevin, and Robert L. Shook. *The Pep Talk*. Nashville: Thomas Nelson, 2008.

Guarino, Lois. *Writing Your Authentic Self*. New York: Dell Publishing,1999.

Kushner, Harold S. *When Bad Things Happen to Good People*. New York: Quill, 2001.

Jeffers, Susan. *Feel the Fear and Do It Anyway*. New York: Ballantine Books, 1987.

Michalko, Michael."Thinking Like a Genius: Eight Strategies Used by the Supercreative, from Aristotle and Leonardo to Einstein and Edison." *The Futurist*, May 1998.

Osteen, Joel. *Your Best Life Now: 7 Steps to Living Your Full Potential*. New York: Warner Faith, 2007.

Pflaum, Bryan. "Learning to Manage Time,"

Stringer, Judy. "Your Job Hunt." Cleveland.com.

University Hospitals. "Maximize Your Memory." UH Marketing Handout.

Yeager, Jeff. *The Ultimate Cheapskate's Road Map to True Riches*. New York: Broadway Books, 2008.

About the Author

Fresh Hope … Cleveland is Nanci's first book but over the years her work and volunteer experiences have provided her with a variety of writing opportunities. She's also written radio shows, press releases, newsletters, sales and fundraiser materials, greeting card copy, health care brochures, and policyholder information. She also enjoyed a position as a ghost writer and a contributing writer *for Northern Ohio Live* magazine's gourmet guide.

While employed in marketing, Nanci spent nearly ten years helping patients and their families with sensitive medical issues. Stepping out of the business world into the arena of books and school bells, Nanci taught language arts for several local school districts. "Helping kids was a wonderful experience. I never laughed so much or knew it could be so much fun and so rewarding to work with students!" she said enthusiastically.

"This book came as a direct response to prayer. I am learning more and more each day what an important vehicle prayer really is and how prayer can unleash God's power and favor in our lives."

Ms. Gravill has a Bachelor of Arts degree in Promotional Communications and three years toward a Bachelor's of Arts degree in Individual & Family Development. Nanci grew up in Bedford, Ohio, and still lives in Northeast Ohio.

Chris Roberts

Chris Roberts designed the great cover for the book. Chris is currently finishing his Bachelor of Arts degree in graphic design with a minor in marketing. He has more than six years experience in design and marketing and has worked with over 40 different clients. His clients have ranged from non-profits organizations, industrial distributors, retail organizations, and science and tech firms. Chris lives near Pittsburgh, Pennsylvania.

Taylor Winteregg

Miss Winteregg is the gifted artist behind Emma, my little field mouse. Emma introduces the social service agencies in this book. Currently, Taylor is working on her associate's degree in Visual Communication Illustration at Cuyahoga Community College in Cleveland. It is her dream to one day illustrate children's books. Envisioning Emma and bringing her to life was an experience she truly enjoyed! We look forward to seeing more of Taylor's work.

With God, all things are possible.

– Amplified Bible (Matthew 19:26)